◆ BUSINESS STATIONERY GRAPHICS 2 ◆

P·I·E BOOKS

BUSINESS STATIONERY GRAPHICS 2

Copyright © 1994 by P·I·E BOOKS

*All right reserved. No part of this publication may be reproduced
in any means, graphic, electronic or mechanical,
including photocopying and recording by an information
storage and retrieval system, without permission
in writing from the publisher.*

*First published in Japan 1994 by : P·I·E BOOKS
Villa Phoenix Suite 407, 4-14-6, Komagome, Toshima-ku,
Tokyo 170, Japan
Tel: 03-3949-5010 Fax: 03-3949-5650
ISBN 4-938586-48-7*

*First published in Germany 1994 by : Nippan
Nippon Shuppan Hanbai Deutschland GmbH
Krefelder Str. 85 D-40549 Düsseldorf 11 (Heerdt) Germany
Tel: 0211-5048089 Fax: 0211-5049326
ISBN 3-910052-37-1*

Printed in Hong Kong

CONTENTS

♦

PREFACE   P. 4

♦

CREATIVE   P. 10

MEDIA / COMMUNICATIONS   P. 92

RETAIL / COMMERCE   P. 114

MANUFACTURING / PRODUCTS   P. 142

PROFESSIONAL   P. 150

SOCIAL / CULTURAL   P. 192

♦

SPECIAL PROGRAM (Fax headers)   P. 209

♦

INDEXES   P. 217

序　文
◆ Preface ◆
Vorwort

序　文

現在は、企業やショップ等を設立する場合に個々のマーケティング・アイデンティティの企画立案と並行して、ロゴやマーク、コーポレートカラーに代表されるビジュアル・アイデンティティを考えてていくことがＣＩ形成の大切な役割であるという意識が定着しているようです。そのようなビジュアル・アイデンティティの中でも、レターヘッド、封筒、名刺といったステーショナリーは、送り手が受け手に対してまず見せたいと思っているイメージを通してコミュニケートする行為を、最も明快にできるチャンスを秘めたグラフィックツールといえるでしょう。

ビジネスで使用されるステーショナリー・システムのアイテムやバリエーションは様々ですが、まず欠かせないレターヘッドの概念を考えてみます。サイズは現在はほとんどがＡ４版、これはＯＡ機器への対応、書類のファイリング等の事務処理においてより効率的なサイズとして世界共通で浸透しつつあります。またレターヘッドはメッセージを書き入れるために存在し、その後折りたたまれて封筒に挿入されるプロセスが待機されている、いわばこれから使われる為のツールです。如何なるメッセージをどのように書き入れるのか、デザインに合う機能的な紙は何か、同様に封筒はどうマッチングさせるか等を考慮する必要性があります。グラフィック・アイテムとしてみた場合、他のものとはビジュアル的に最終ではない点において特異な存在と言えます。言い換えれば、その構成要素や諸事情に規制の多いのがレターヘッドです。

本書がVol.1に引き続き２を出版することになったポイントにはまず、社会背景及びビジネスのあり方が変容し、それに伴いステーショナリー・デザインもリニューアルし変わってきているということがあります。加えて、Vol.1以上に多彩な国々の作品を掲載しています。その数は１７か国、それぞれの国民性や文化、デザイン傾向の違いなどを楽しみながらイマジネーションを刺激できるのではないでしょうか。もう一つ、今回はスペシャルプログラムと銘打ってFax用紙を紹介しています。ステーショナリーの中で例えばレターヘッドとFax用紙を比較してみますと、本来の目的及びふさわしい内容において双方は対極の違いを備えており、デザイン的には前者の方がはるかに時間とコストをかけて制作されていることは顕著です。が、Faxにおいてはワールドワイドな視野から今後さらに合理的になるであろうビジネス・コミュニケーションの可能性を多大に持ち合わせています。すなわち、レターヘッド・デザインが数年で変わっていったのと同様に、Fax用紙のデザインに関する認識と理解はますます深まっていくのではないかと推測されます。これらの事情に注目して、"Fax headers"のプログラムを楽しみながら見て触発されてください。現状ではモノクロが主体であり、簡素なフォルムながらも斬新な要素を含んでいる作品を本書ではチョイスしてみました。おそらく初めての試みであろう当プログラムが、これからのビジネス・ステーショナリー・アイデンティティのサポートとなれば幸いです。また印刷技術の発達により、様々な特殊効果を使った新しいタイプのステーショナリーも数多く登場しています。本書で掲載している作品の中からそのテクニックのいくつかを列記してみますと、盛り上げ印刷、箔押し、型押し（エンボス）、メタリック・インク、ラバースタンプ、ニス状の上塗り、型抜き等があります。またテクニックと相乗して、紙の扱いや紙質の選び方もステーショナリーを構成する大切な要素として見逃せません。ベースに薄く色柄をひいたもの、裏面全体をプリントしたもの、グラデーショントーン使い等のデザイン効果や、和紙、トレーシングペーパー、表裏の色が違う紙等、数々の表情のある紙を選んでいます。実際現物の感触をお届けできないのが残念な所ですが、それらの新鮮なアイデアソースは、もちろんクライアントの事業内容がベースとなっています。本書はクライアントの業種で大きくグルーピングし、個々のステーショナリーに事業内容を表記してあります。

ビジネス・ステーショナリーにおいての優れたデザインは、先に述べたようにクライアントのビジュアル・アイデンティティ意向に伴って、様々な制約のある中でどれだけ機能的なものに仕上げるかというのが最大のポイントです。これは、パーソナリティの表現方法も然り、ビジネスにおいてそれぞれのステーショナリーの扱いをきちんと押さえた上で、コミュニケーション・ツールとしてデザインをどう反映させるかということです。本書をご覧いただく読者の方々が、これから登場するステーショナリー・グラフィックスのオリジナリティと美しさを感じとるのと同時にその機能美も理解していただけることを期待しています。

ピエ・ブックス編集部

Preface

Today, Almost everyone is aware of the importance of creating a strong visual identity in the public mind. Logos, trademarks, corporate colors and so on are among the primary tools in this undertaking, along with the more conventional approach of establishing specific, individual identities for given target markets. Stationery, such as letter heads, envelopes and business cards, is a system of communication tools that constitutes a key element in the making of a corporate identity. And because stationery incorporates graphic tools, it has the potential to carry an image of the sender directly and intimately to the recipient.

There is a wonderful diversity of items included in business stationery systems used today. Consider for a moment the letterhead, which is still probably the anchor of any stationery system. The most common size is A4, now widely used all over the world. This international standard has proven efficient for various applications, including use in OA devices, filing, correspondence and so forth. The letterhead exists to carry a message and, inherent in the object, there is the process, whereby it is written on, folded and inserted into an envelope. In other words, the letterhead is nothing before it is used, but when it's time comes, the letterhead is more than just the sum of its parts. The unique quality of the letterhead is that, visually speaking, it is not a final product; it is the user who puts the finishing touches on it. Thus, it is necessary for the designer of a letterhead to consider how the message will be presented - the format and style of the actual words that will be written on the page, the type of paper that will optimize the function of the letter and so on. Also, how will it coordinate with the envelope and other elements in the stationery system?

One of the reasons we decided to produce Volume 2 of Business Stationery Graphics, after the success of Volume 1, is that since that first issue was published, both the social background and the business community have undergone a major shift, and we have discovered that stationery design on the whole has moved as well; it has been renewed. Volume 2 also carries graphic design works from a broader field than Volume 1; seventeen countries are represented in this volume. We are confident that these work, collected from around the world, will move, delight and inspire you. You will appreciate the fine differences in national characteristics, cultural influences and design inclinations among these pieces. Another special feature of this volume is the inclusion of fax cover sheets.

Among the various stationery items, notice that letterheads and fax cover sheets are quite the contrary of each other in their original objectives and the contents they are supposed to carry. From a design point of view, the former often carries very distinctly higher "production values" than does its cousin, the fax cover sheet. We can easily imagine, however, that these rather utilitarian, monochrome designs will blossom in the future, somewhat the way letterhead design has over the past couple of decades. The importance of the fax cover sheet as a front line of visual communication is being recognized even now, and a revolution is already underway. Keeping these points in mind, we hope you will enjoy our "Fax headers" feature. Fax cover sheet design is generally in monochrome, and we selected designs with relatively simple formats but which were, nevertheless, daring in some way. This feature is probably the first of a kind, and we hope will serve to invigorate the development of new possibilities in business stationery.

Another point to be noted is that, with advances in state of the art printing technology, we are seeing numerous new types of stationery items that use spectacular special effects. To list a few that are shown here, you will see thermography, foil stamping, embossing, metallic inks, rubber stamps, varnishing and engraving. In happy collaboration with all this technology is the paper itself; and the choice of paper stock continues to be the foundation of any stationery system. The items shown in this book employ all manner of media, including screen tints, paper with printing covering the entire back surface and design effects such as tone gradation. We are also seeing various types and textures of paper such as traditional rice paper, tracing paper and paper with different colors on front and back. We have done our best to bring you the actual texture of these tactile treats by sparing nothing in our reproduction techniques.

The best identities are always based upon the clients' actual business activities. In this volume, the works are grouped according to the type of business the client is engaged in, and this information is clearly indicated for each item.

The most crucial point in any design for business stationery is its serviceability; is it functional and, at the same time, does it faithfully reflect the visual identity of the client? Just as in the expression of individual personalities, the heart of the matter is how well the design can facilitate communication of a specific, individual message within the scheme of an overall, coordinated framework.

Finally, it is our hope for this volume, that it will help our readers better appreciate the beauty of functionality while enjoying the artistic verve of the stationery graphics contained here.

P·I·E BOOKS Editorial Department

Vorwort

Heute ist fast jedem die Bedeutung einer starken visuellen Identität im öffentlichen Bewußtsein bekannt und Logos, Warenzeichen, Firmenfarben und dergleichen sind die wichtigsten Werkzeuge in diesem Unterfangen im Einklang mit konventionellem Ansatz um unverwechselbare, individuelle Identitäten in einem vorgegebenen Marktziel zu etablieren. Geschäftsdrucksachen wie Briefbogen, Umschläge und Visitenkarten bilden ein System von kommunikativen Medien, das die Schlüsselposition bei der Einrichtung einer Corporate Identity besetzt. Und weil Geschäftsdrucksachen graphische Elemente inkorporieren haben sie das Potential, das Image des Senders direkt und unmittelbar zum Empfänger zu transportieren.

Es gibt mittlerweile eine wunderbare Vielfalt im Bereich Geschäftsdrucksachen. Denken Sie einmal an den Briefbogen, der nach wie vor der Schwerpunkt von Geschäftsdrucksachen ist. DinA 4 ist mittlerweile das gebräuchlichste Format. Dieser internationale Standard zeigt sich bei unterschiedlichsten Anwendungen als sehr effektiv inklusive in der Anwendung aller Formen von Computern, Ablage, Korrespondenz usw. Der Briefbogen existiert um eine Nachricht zu transportieren und inkorporiert bereits den Prozess des Beschreibens, Faltens und Einkouvertierens. In anderen Worten ist der Briefbogen ein Nichts bevor er verwendet wird und wenn seine Zeit gekommen ist, mehr als die Summe der Teile. Die einzigartige Eigenschaft des Briefbogens ist daher, im visuellen Kontext, daß er kein endgültiges Produkt ist: wer ihn verwendet, fügt die letzten Feinheiten hinzu. Daher kann der Designer nicht außer Acht lassen, wie die Nachricht präsentiert werden wird - das Format und der Schriftstil, mit dem die Seite dann tatsächlich beschrieben wird, die Papiersorte, die die Funktion des Briefes optimieren soll usw. Natürlich ist auch zu beachten, wie die Koordination mit dem Umschlag und anderen Bestandteilen der Geschäftsausstattung vorsich geht.

Einer der Gründe, warum wir uns mit BUSINESS STATIONARY GRAPHICS 2 zur Fortsetzung des erfolgreichen ersten Bandes entschlossen haben ist, daß sich seit der Veröffentlichung des ersten Bandes sowohl der soziale Hintergrund und die Geschäftswelt massiv verändert haben, und wir beobachten konnten, daß die Geschäftsdrucksachen in gleichem Maße verändert und oftmals erneuert wurden. Band 2 reflektiert außerdem eine Auswahl von Designs, die mit insgesamt 17 Herkunftsländern wesentlich breiter angelegt ist. Wir sind sicher, daß sich diese internationalen Arbeiten dazu eignen, Sie zu motivieren, zu erfreuen und zu inspirieren.

Sicherlich werden Sie die feinen Nuancen in nationalem Charakter, kulturellen Einflüssen und Designströmungen zu schätzen wissen. Eine weitere Besonderheit ist die Berücksichtigung von Telefax-Deckblättern.

Unter den verschiedenen Bestandteilen der Geschäftsdrucksachen sind Briefbogen und Telefax-Deckblatt sicherlich - unter Berücksichtigung von Form und Inhalt - das Paar mit den größten Gesätzlichkeiten. Unter Designgesichtspunkten ist der Briefbogen sicherlich oft mit dem größten Produktionswert ausgestattet, als das Fax-Deckblatt. Aber wir können uns gut vorstellen, daß diese zweckorientierten, einfarbigen Designs sich in Zukunft ebenso entwickeln werden wie Briefbögen in den letzten Jahrzehnten. Die Bedeutung das Fax-Deckblattes als vorderste Linie der Kommunikation wird eigentlich gerade jetzt erst entdeckt, und das hat die Designs schon revolutioniert. Unter diesen Gesichtspunkten hoffen wir, daß die Sektion "Telefax-Deckblätter" Sie sowohl anregen als auch informieren wird. Telefax-Deckblätter sind bisher generell einfarbig und wir haben relativ einfache Formate ausgewählt, die vom Design her jedoch recht kühn sind. Diese Sektion ist wahrscheinlich die erste ihrer Art, und wir hoffen, daß sie Ihnen hilft, neue Bereiche in der Gestaltung von Geschäftapapieren zu entdecken.

Eine weitere Besonderheit ist, daß wir den Fortschritten in der Drucktechnik Rechnung zu tragen hatten, und wir stellen zahlreiche Geschäftsdrucksachen mit speziellen Effekten vor. Um nur einige Techniken zu nennen: Thermographie, Folienprägung, Prägung, Metallic-Druckfarben, Flexdruck, Lackierung und Stahl (Kupfer) - Stich. In erfreulicher Zusammenarbeit mit diesen Techniken finden sich die verwendeten Papiere, und die Papierwahl wird immer stärker zum ausschlaggebenden Kriterium bei Geschäftspapieren. Die vorgestellten Objekte zeigen eine große Vielfalt u.a. Siebdruck, rückseitig vollflächig bedruckte Papier - oder Farbverläufe. Wir sehen auch verschiedenste Arten von Texturen von Papier von traditionellen Sorten aus Reisstroh zu Zeichenpapier und Papieren mit unterschiedlich gefärbten Vorder - und Rückseiten. Wir haben versucht, diese Effekte und faktilen Eigenschaften mit der besten Reproduktionstechnik sichtbar und nachvollziehbar zu machen.

Die erfolgreichsten Firmenidentitäten basieren in der Regel immer auf den tatsächlichen Geschäftsaktivitäten des Kunden. In diesem Band sind die Arbeiten nach Geschäftsbereichen gegliedert und jedes objekt ist mit der entsprechenden Information versehen.

Der ausschlaggebende Punkt bei jedem Design von Geschäftsdrucksachen ist die Benutzbarkeit, ist sie funktional und - gleich - zeitig - reflektiert sie die visuelle Identität des Auftraggebers? Ebenso wie der individuelle, persönliche Ausdruck, ist der Kernpunkt, wie das Design die Kommunikation einer spezifischen individuellen Nachricht in einem allgegenwärtigen, koordinierten Rahmen unterstützt.

Abschließend ist es unsere Hoffnung für diesen Band, daß er den Lesern hilft, die Schönheit der Funktionalität zu erkennen und gleichzeitig die künstlerische Verve der vorgestellten Geschäftsdrucksacher zu genießen.

Die Herausgeber von P·I·E BOOKS

Editorial Notes

Client , Client's Company Type ,
Submitor's Nationality ,Year of Completion

CD:Creative Director
AD:Art Director
D:Designer
P:Photographer
I:Illustrator
CW:Copy Writer
DF:Design Firm

Special Effects:Special Finishing Processes Used.
Except for `Client' entries,the words "Company Limited" and
"Incorporated" have been omitted from the credits in this book.
本文クレジット中、作品のクライアントを除く
会社名については株式（有限）会社、
Company Limited, Incorporated 等の表記を省略した。

BUSINESS STATIONERY GRAPHICS

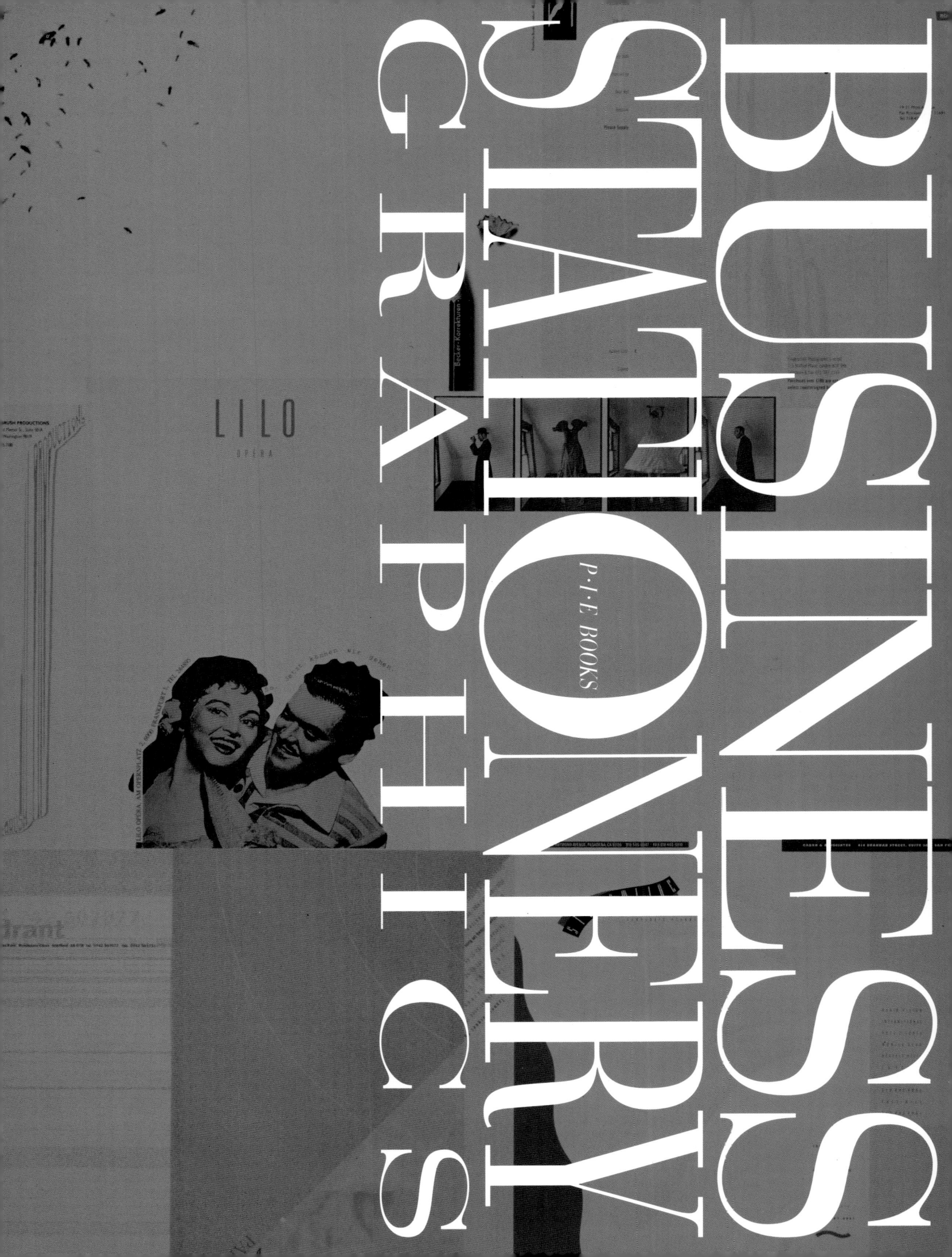

P·I·E BOOKS

• CREATIVE •

THE DESIGNERS REPUBLIC   Graphic Design and Art Direction   グラフィックデザイン、アートディレクション   UK 1991
AD, D: The Designers Republic   D: Mark Ross / Peter Ward   DF: The Designers Republic

• CREATIVE •

DESIGNERS COMPANY　Graphic Design　グラフィックデザイン　THE NETHERLANDS　1993　AD, D: Marcel Gort　DF: Designers Company

• C R E A T I V E •

I COMME IMAGE Graphic Design　グラフィックデザイン　FRANCE 1990 AD, D: Jsan Jacques Tachdjian DF: I Comme Image

• CREATIVE •

KINEMA MOON DESIGNING   Graphic Design   グラフィックデザイン   JAPAN   1993   AD: Yuichi Nakagawa   D: Sachiko Kitani   DF: Kinema Moon Designing

• C R E A T I V E •

MIKE SALISBURY COMMUNICATIONS Graphic Design グラフィックデザイン USA 1993 AD: Mike Salisbury D, I: Regina Grosveld DF: Mike Salisbury Communications

• CREATIVE •

ESQUISSE INC. Goods Design グッズデザイン JAPAN AD, D: Tatsuomi Majima ARTIST: Bob Zoell DF: Majima Design

• 15 •

• CREATIVE •

RENO DESIGN GROUP Graphic Design and Consultancy グラフィックデザイン、コンサルタント AUSTRALIA 1990 AD, D: Graham Rendoth CW: Reno Design Group DF: Reno Design Group

• CREATIVE •

REMY PAGART Architecture and Interior Design 建築設計、インテリアデザイン FRANCE 1992 AD, D: Jean Jacques Tachdjian DF: I Comme Image
CHARLES S. ANDERSON DESIGN COMPANY Graphic Design グラフィックデザイン USA 1991 AD, D: Todd Hauswirth DF: Charles S. Anderson Design

• CREATIVE •

MELIA DESIGN GROUP Graphic Design グラフィックデザイン USA 1990 AD, D: P. Michael Melia D: Mark Skingcuber / Jordan Louie DF: Melia Design Group
Special Effects: Trademark and margin have been embossed. マークと中の枠が型押しされている。

• CREATIVE •

THE DESIGN OFFICE OF WONG & YEO Graphic Design グラフィックデザイン USA 1993 AD, D: Hock Wah Yeo D: Cary Chiao DF: The Design Office of Wong & Yeo
Special Effects: Striped metallic paper has been used. ストライプの入ったメタリック紙を使用。

PLAZA / VAN DER SCHANS Graphic and Industrial Design グラフィック、工業デザイン THE NETHERLANDS 1993 CD: Robert van Rixlel DF: Plaza Ontwerpers

◆ CREATIVE ◆

· 21 ·

• CREATIVE •

GULLIVER CO., LTD.   Printing   プリンティング   JAPAN 1992   CD: Seiji Koseki   AD: Tatsuomi Majima   D: 1. Yukio Ikoma / 2. Masami Shimizu

• CREATIVE •

GULLIVER CO., LTD.   Printing   プリンティング   JAPAN   1992   CD: Seiji Koseki   AD: Tatsuomi Majima   D: 1. Yoshiro Kajitani / 2. Shin Matsunaga

• 25 •

• C R E A T I V E •

EYE STUDIO   Photography / Design   写真 / デザイン   HONG KONG   1992   AD, D: Ching Lai Shan   P: Kam Ming, Ng   DF: Eye Studio

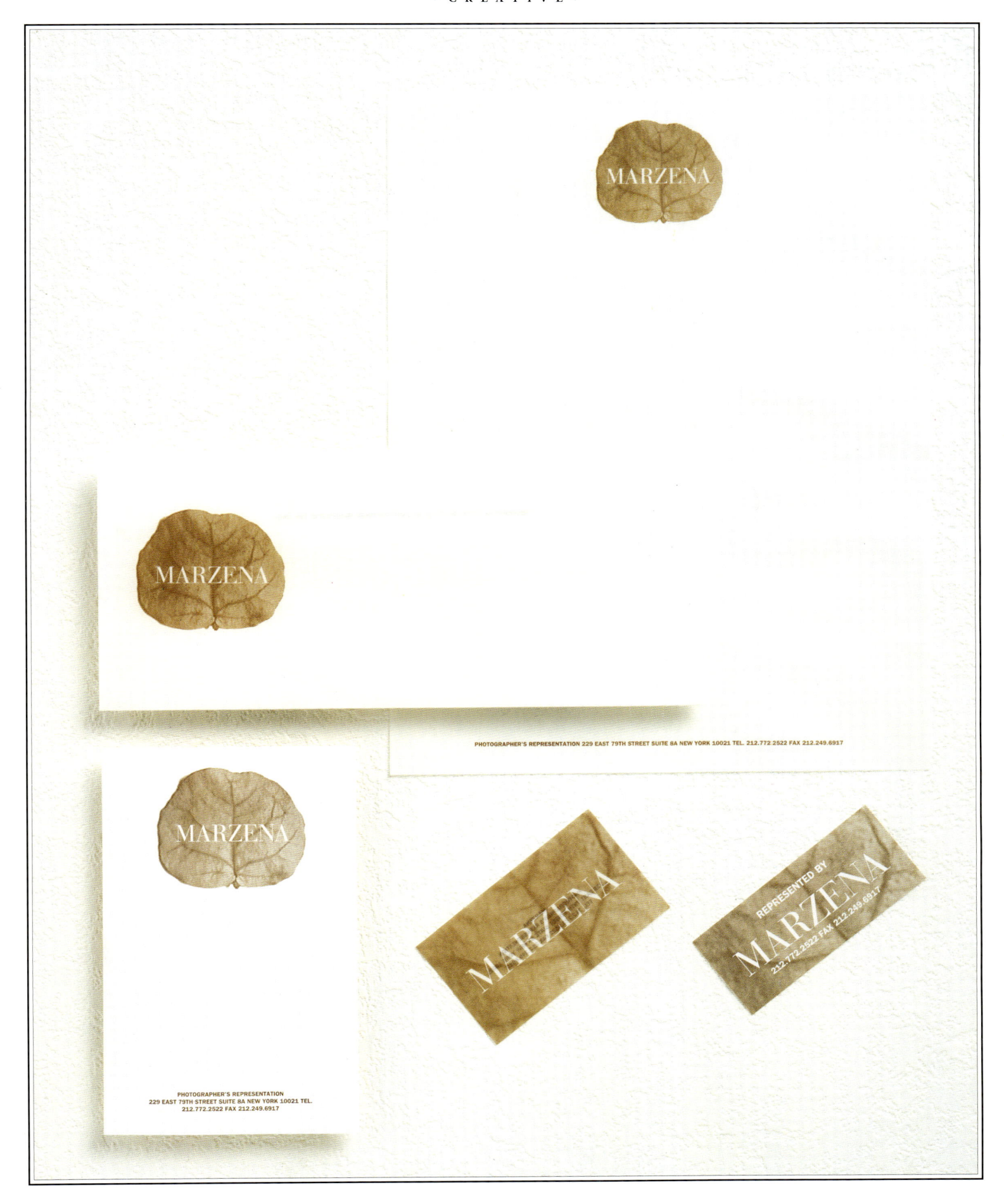

MARZENA Photographer's Representation 写真家の代理・演出 USA 1992 CD: Robert Bergman-Ungar D: Liong The

• CREATIVE •

CESAR RUBIO PHOTOGRAPHY   Photographic Studio   写真スタジオ   USA 1992   D: Raul Cabra   P: Cesar Rubio   DF: Cabra Diseño

• CREATIVE •

PENDULUM DESIGN Graphic Communication グラフィックデザイン AUSTRALIA 1993 AD: John Sellitto D: David Blyth P: Tim Scott

• CREATIVE •

ART KANE   Photographer   写真家   USA 1991   AD, P: Art Kane   AD, D: Miho   DF: Miho

• CREATIVE •

RYOICHI SAITO   Photographer   写真家   JAPAN   AD, D: Tatsuomi Majima   P: Ryoichi Saito   DF: Majima Design

SHIN SUGINO PHOTOGRAPHY　Photographer　写真家　CANADA　1991　AD, D: Del Terrelonge　P: Shin Sugino　DF: Terrelonge Design

• CREATIVE •

· 33 ·

• CREATIVE •

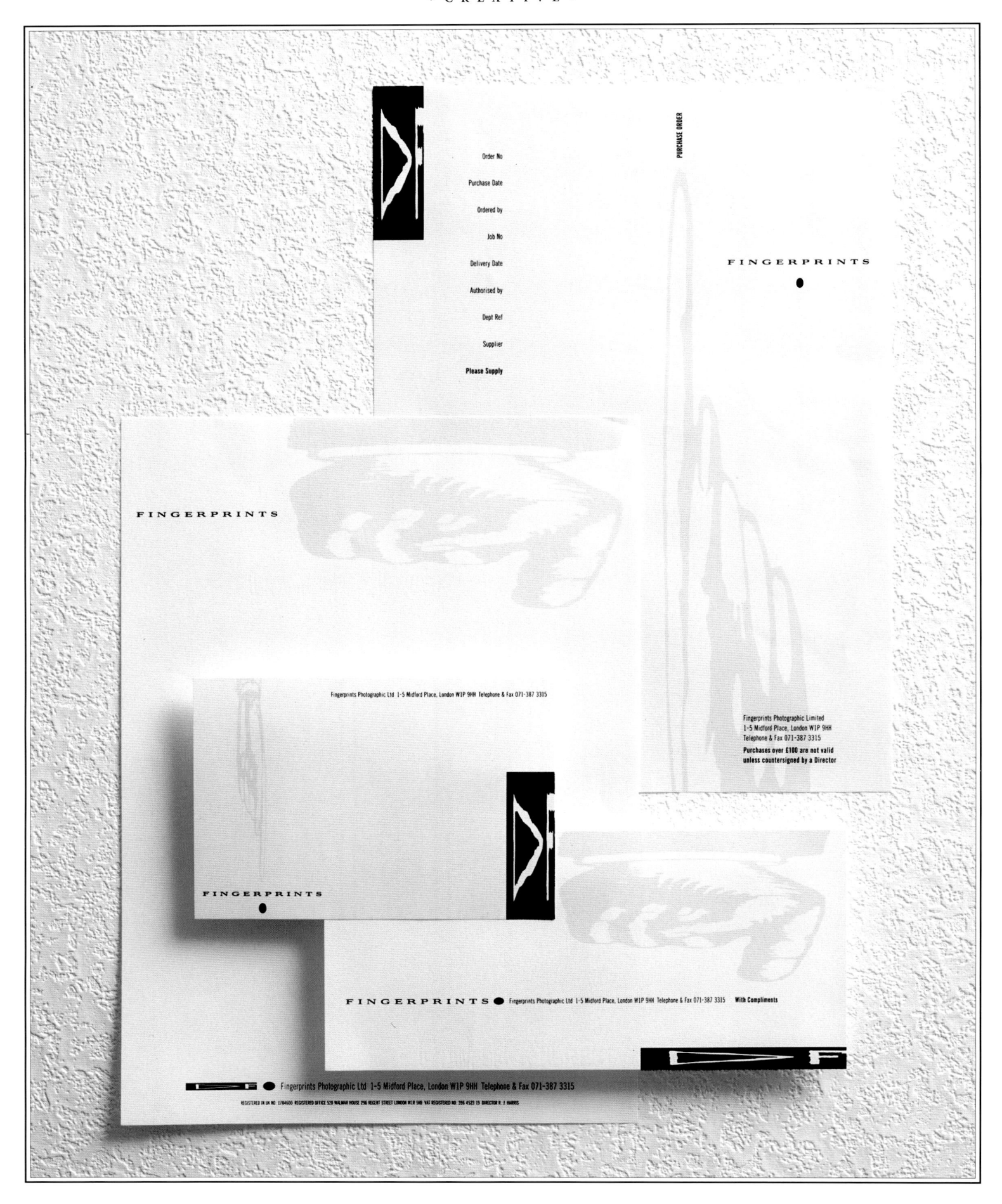

FINGERPRINTS PHOTOGRAPHIC LIMITED   Photographic Services   写真サービス   UK 1989   AD, D, I: Glenn Hilling   DF: Glenn Hilling

• CREATIVE •

CALLAHAN & COMPANY Photographic Services 写真サービス USA 1987 AD, D, P: Dianne Yanovick DF: Yanovick & Associates

• CREATIVE •

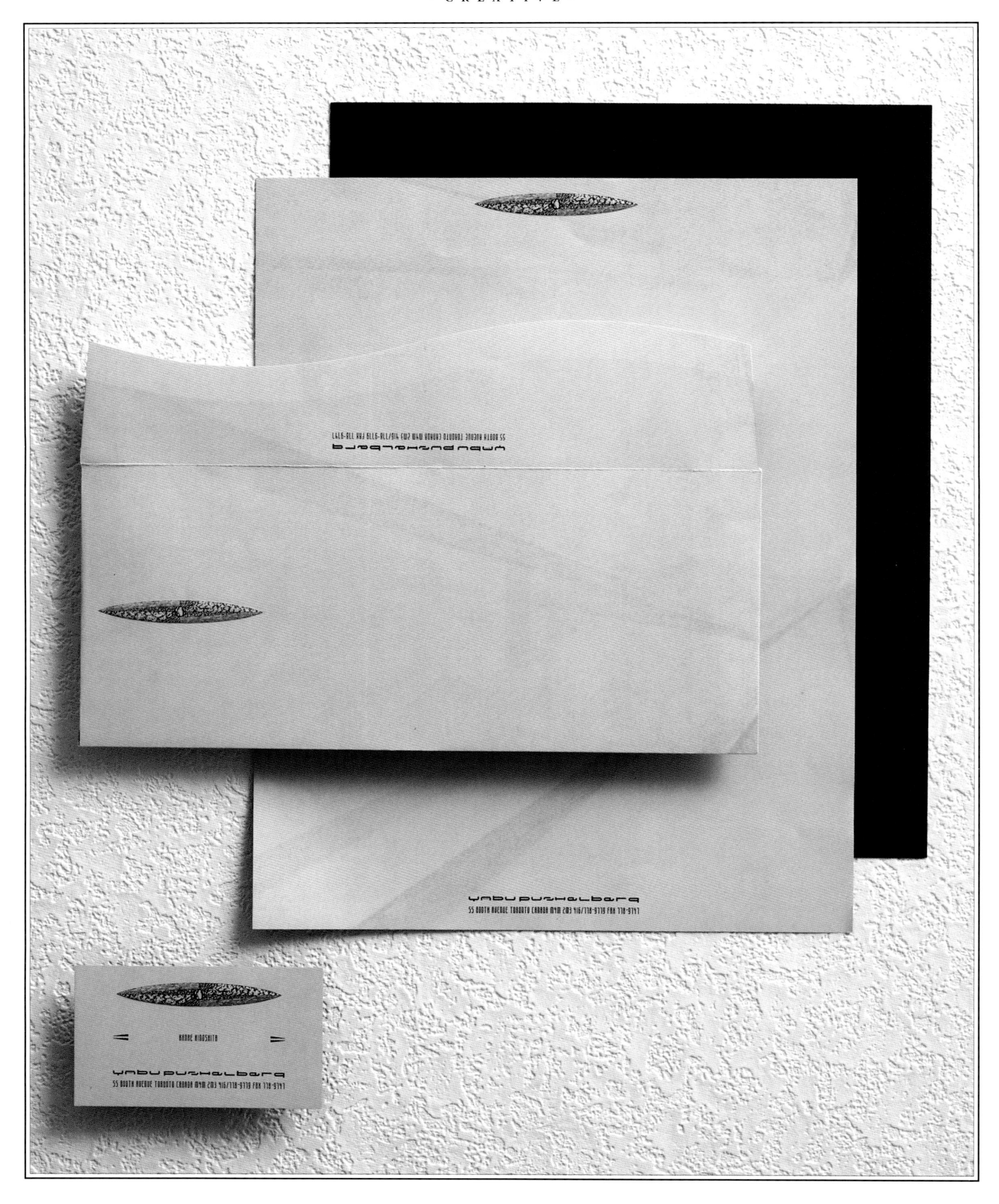

YABU PUSHELBERG   Interior Design   インテリアデザイン   CANADA   1990   AD, D: Del Terrelonge   DF: Terrelonge Design
Special Effects: Trademark has been embossed.   マークが型押しされている。

• CREATIVE •

ROBERT BERGMAN-UNGAR　Art Direction　アートディレクション　USA　1993　CD: Robert Bergman-Ungar　D: Liong The

• C R E A T I V E •

H. M. BRANDSTON & PARTNERS Lighting Design 照明デザイン USA 1991 AD, D: Richard Poulin DF: Richard Poulin Design Group
Special Effects: Clear varnish has been used for the upper portion. 上部の枠内にニス状の上塗りをしてある。
RICK WAHLSTROM Photographer 写真家 USA 1986 AD, D: Jennifer Morla Special Effects: Logomark has been embossed. マークが型押しされている。

• C R E A T I V E •

STUDIO SEIREENI   Design and Advertising   デザイン、広告   USA 1991   CD: Richard Seireeni   AD, D: Romane Cameron   P, I: Geof Kern   DF: Studio Seireeni

ELLEN ROSENBERG   Interior Design   インテリアデザイン   USA 1993   D: Jilly Simons / Cindy Chang   DF: Concrete, Chicago

• CREATIVE •

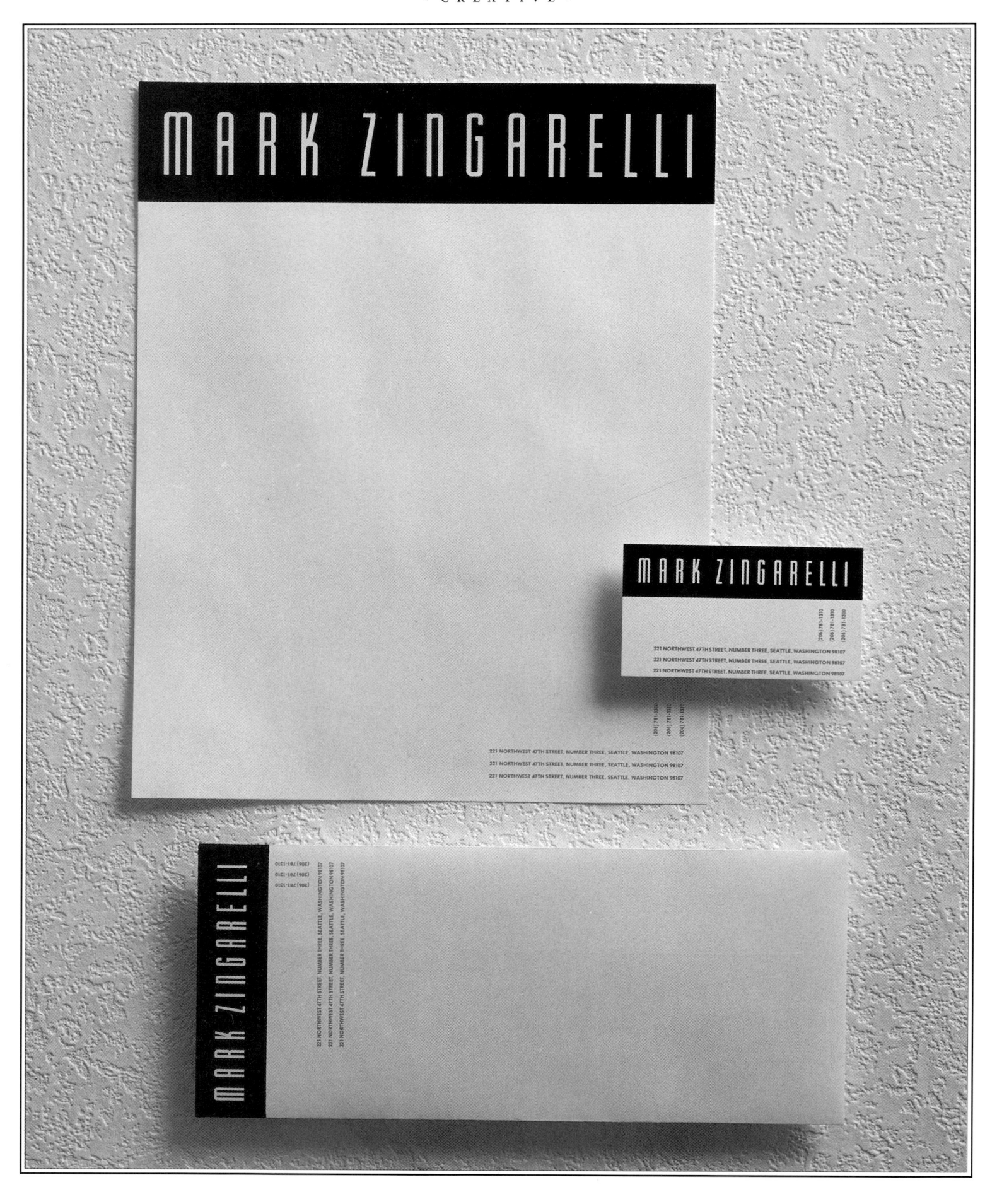

MARK ZINGARELLI Illustrator イラストレーター USA 1989 AD, D, P, I, CW: Art Chantry DF: Art Chantry Design

• CREATIVE •

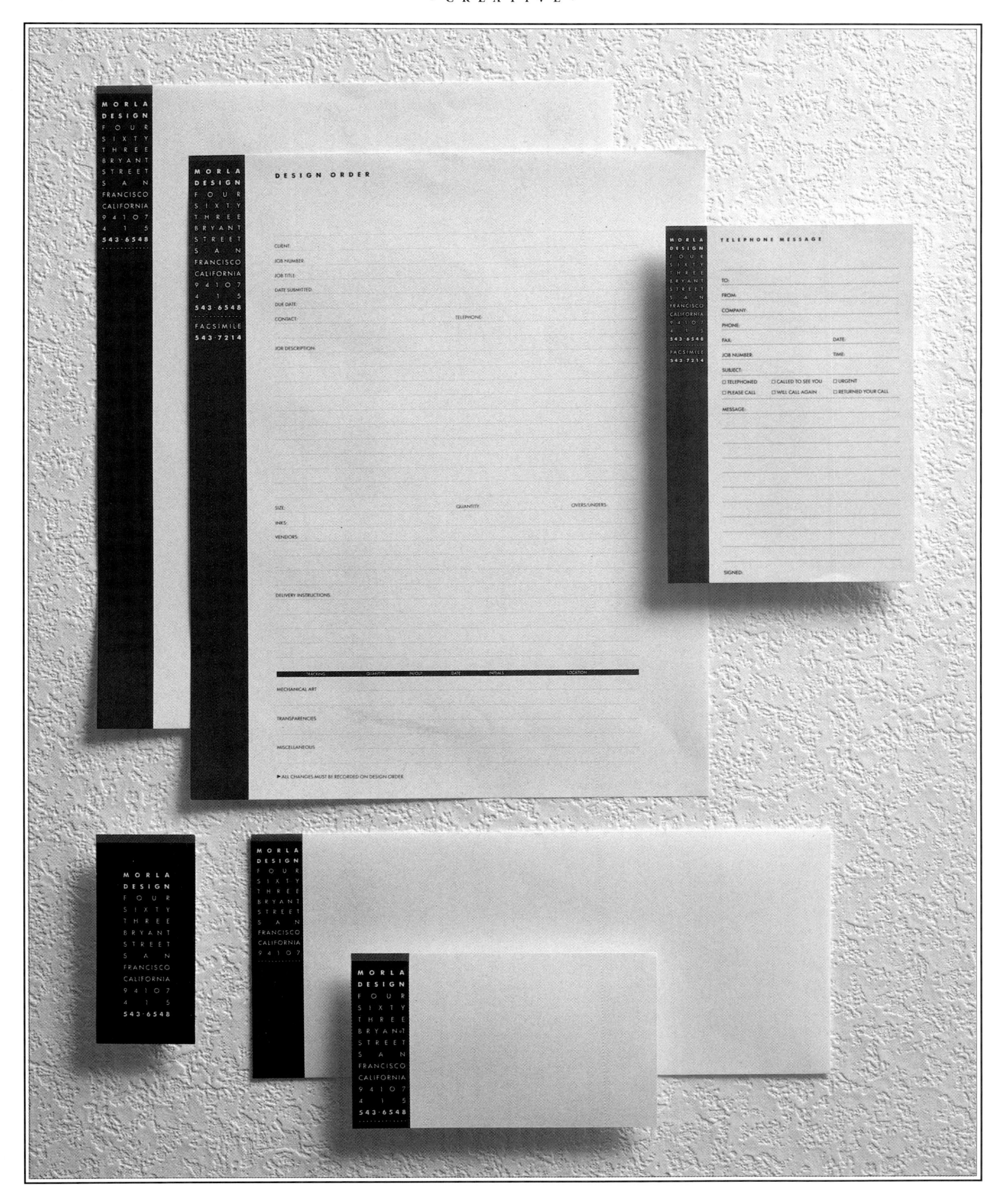

MORLA DESIGN Graphic Design グラフィックデザイン USA 1987 AD, D, CW: Jennifer Morla CW: Michelle Mitchell

• CREATIVE •

CAHAN & ASSOCIATES Graphic Design   グラフィックデザイン   USA 1990   AD: Bill Cahan   D, I: Talin Gureghian / Stuart Flake   DF: Cahan & Associates

• CREATIVE •

FORSYTHE DESIGN　Graphic Design　グラフィックデザイン　USA　1989　AD, D: Kathleen Forsythe　D: Julie Steinhilber　DF: Forsythe Design

• C R E A T I V E •

SAGMEISTER GRAPHICS VIENNA　Graphic Design　グラフィックデザイン　HONG KONG　1990　AD, D: Stefan Sagmeister　DF: Sagmeister Graphics

• CREATIVE •

TOM SCHIERLITZ Photographer 写真家 HONG KONG 1989 AD, D: Stefan Sagmeister DF: Sagmeister Graphics

• CREATIVE •

CLIF SPARKMAN Photographer 写真家 USA 1991 AD, D: P. Michael Melia DF: Melia Design Group

FHA DESIGN Graphic Design グラフィックデザイン AUSTRALIA 1993 AD, D: Richard Henderson D: Julia Jarvis DF: FHA Design Australia

• C R E A T I V E •

M. E. DESIGN, LOS ANGELES　Design　デザイン　USA　1986　AD, D: Rebeca Méndez

ABO ARCHITECTS　Architecture　建築設計　USA　1992　AD, D: David Warren　DF: David Warren Design

• 49 •

• CREATIVE •

NUMBER ONE DESIGN OFFICE　Graphic Design　グラフィックデザイン　JAPAN　1991　AD,D: Kenichi Samura　DF: Number One Design Office

• C R E A T I V E •

STEWART TILGER Photography 写真 USA 1991 AD, D: John Hornall D: David Bates DF: Hornall Anderson Design Works

• CREATIVE •

LATCHEZAR BOYADJIEV Art Glass Design アートガラス・デザイン USA 1992 AD, D: Iva Frank DF: Iva Frank Graphic Design
REKTA REKLAM TASARIM Advertising and Design 広告、デザイン TURKEY 1991 AD: Hakan Poroy D: Goskun Türk DF: Rekta Reklam Tasarim

ALFALFA　Children's Fashion Photography　子供のファッション写真　UK　1990　AD, D: Teresa Roviras　DF: Teresa Roviras
Special Effects: Positive film has been pasted on.　ポジフィルムが貼られている。

• CREATIVE •

JOE TRELEVEN Photographic Studio 写真スタジオ USA 1991 AD, D: Todd Nesser DF: McCool & Company
ART DIRECTORS CLUB OF METROPOLITAN WASHINGTON Art Direction アートディレクション USA 1992 AD, D: Supon Phornirunlit P: Barry Myer DF: Supon Design Group

• 54 •

• CREATIVE •

LEONARD CURRIE DESIGN Typographic Design タイポグラフィック・デザイン UK 1989 D, TYPOGRAPHER: Leonard Currie DF: Leonard Currie Design
ALLYSON ANTHONY Stylist スタイリスト USA 1990 AD, D: Jennifer Morla DF: Morla Design

• CREATIVE •

THE DESIGN OFFICE, INC. Graphic Design グラフィックデザイン USA 1987 D: Joseph H. Feigenbaum DF: The Design Office

• CREATIVE •

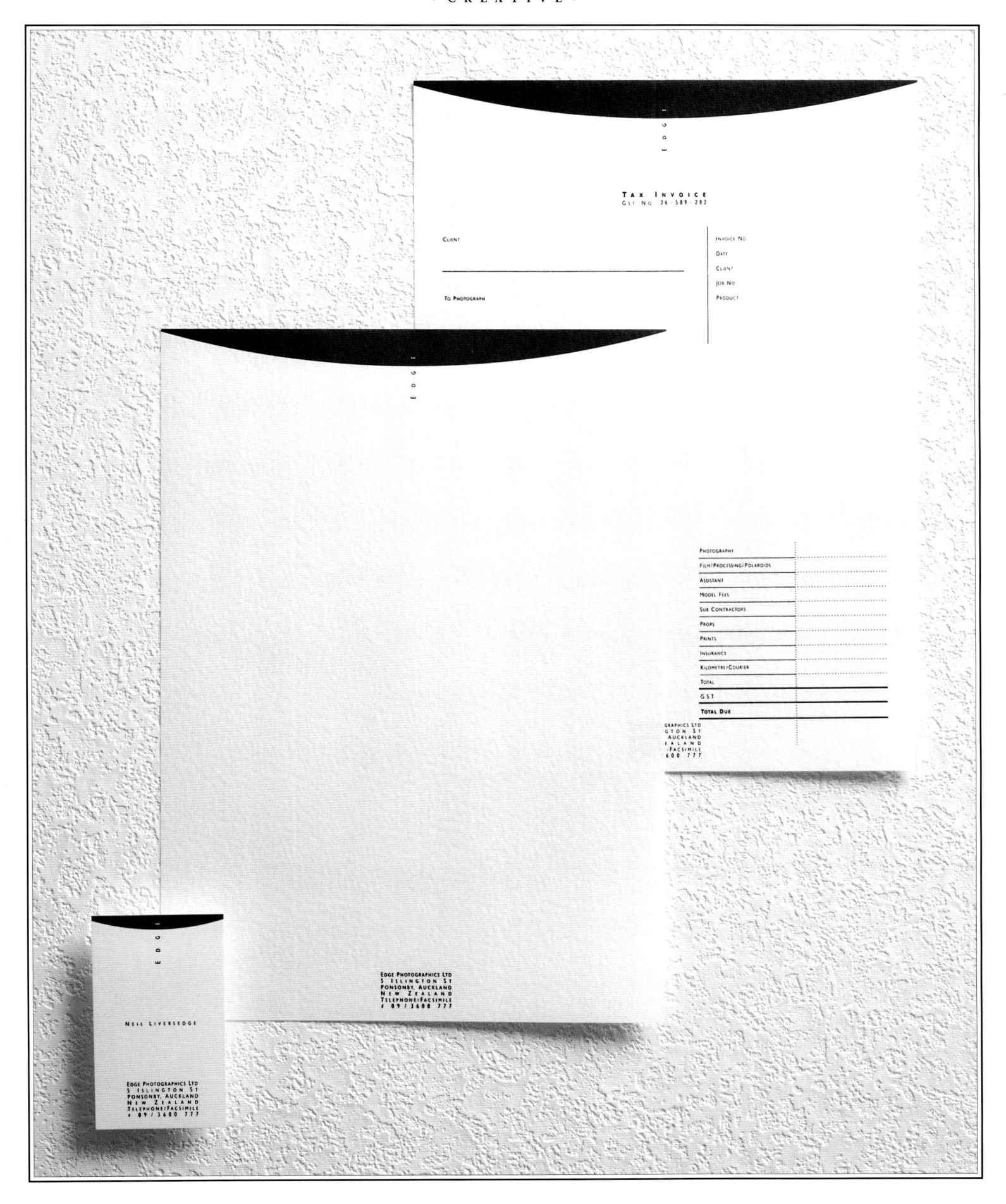

EDGE PHOTOGRAPHY Photographer 写真家 NEW ZEALAND 1991 AD, D: Peter Roband P: Neil Liversedge DF: Peter Haythornthwaite Design

• C R E A T I V E •

ANDY IP   Design   デザイン   CANADA   D, I: Andy Ip

LINDSTROM PHOTOGRAPHY   Commercial Photography   商業写真   USA   D, I: Lauren Smith   DF: Lauren Smith Design

• CREATIVE •

KODAK PHOTO SERVICE Professional Portrait Photographs ポートレイト専門写真 AUSTRIA 1992 AD, D, I, CW: Sigi Ramoser DF: Sigi Ramoser
TADEUSZ PIECHURA Graphic Design グラフィックデザイン POLAND 1989 AD, D: Tadeusz Piechura DF: Aterier Tadeusz Piechura

• C R E A T I V E •

HIGGINS DESIGN Graphic Design グラフィックデザイン USA 1992 CD, D: Jane Higgins DF: Higgins Design
UWE STEINMAYER Graphic Design グラフィックデザイン GERMANY 1992 AD, D: Uwe Steinmayer

• C R E A T I V E •

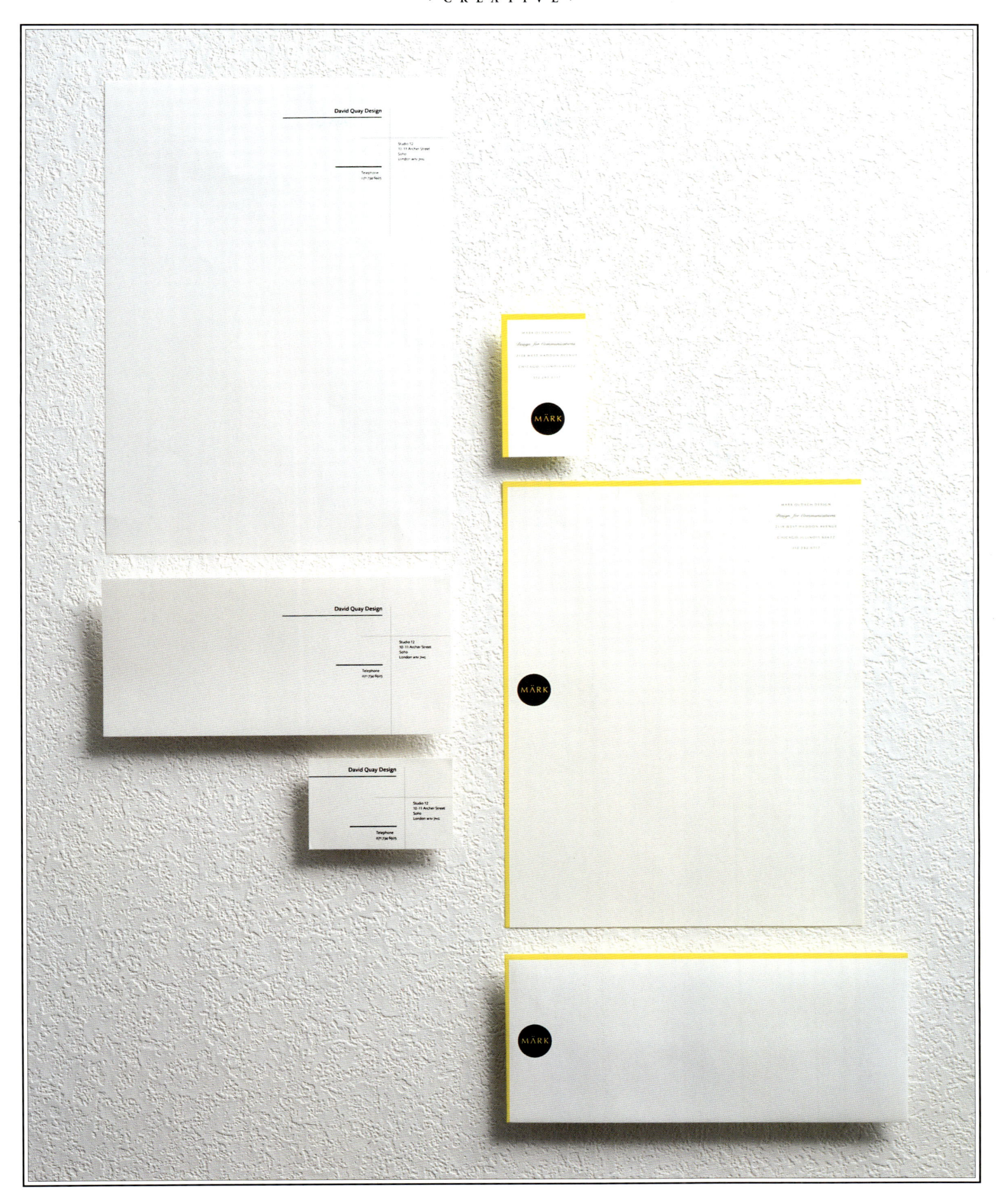

DAVID QUAY DESIGN Design デザイン UK 1991 D: David Quay DF: David Quay Design
MARK OLDACH DESIGN Graphic Design グラフィックデザイン USA 1990 AD, D: Mark Oldach DF: Mark Oldach Design

• CREATIVE •

LIMAGE DANGEREUSE BV　Graphic Design　グラフィックデザイン　THE NETHERLANDS　1991
CD: Arie V Baarle　AD: Theo Seesing　D, I: Limage Dangereuse　CW: Taco Sipma　DF: Limage Dangereuse

• CREATIVE •

WATERS DESIGN ASSOCIATES, INC. Graphic Design グラフィックデザイン USA AD, D: John Waters D, I: Dana Gonsalves DF: Waters Design Associates

• CREATIVE •

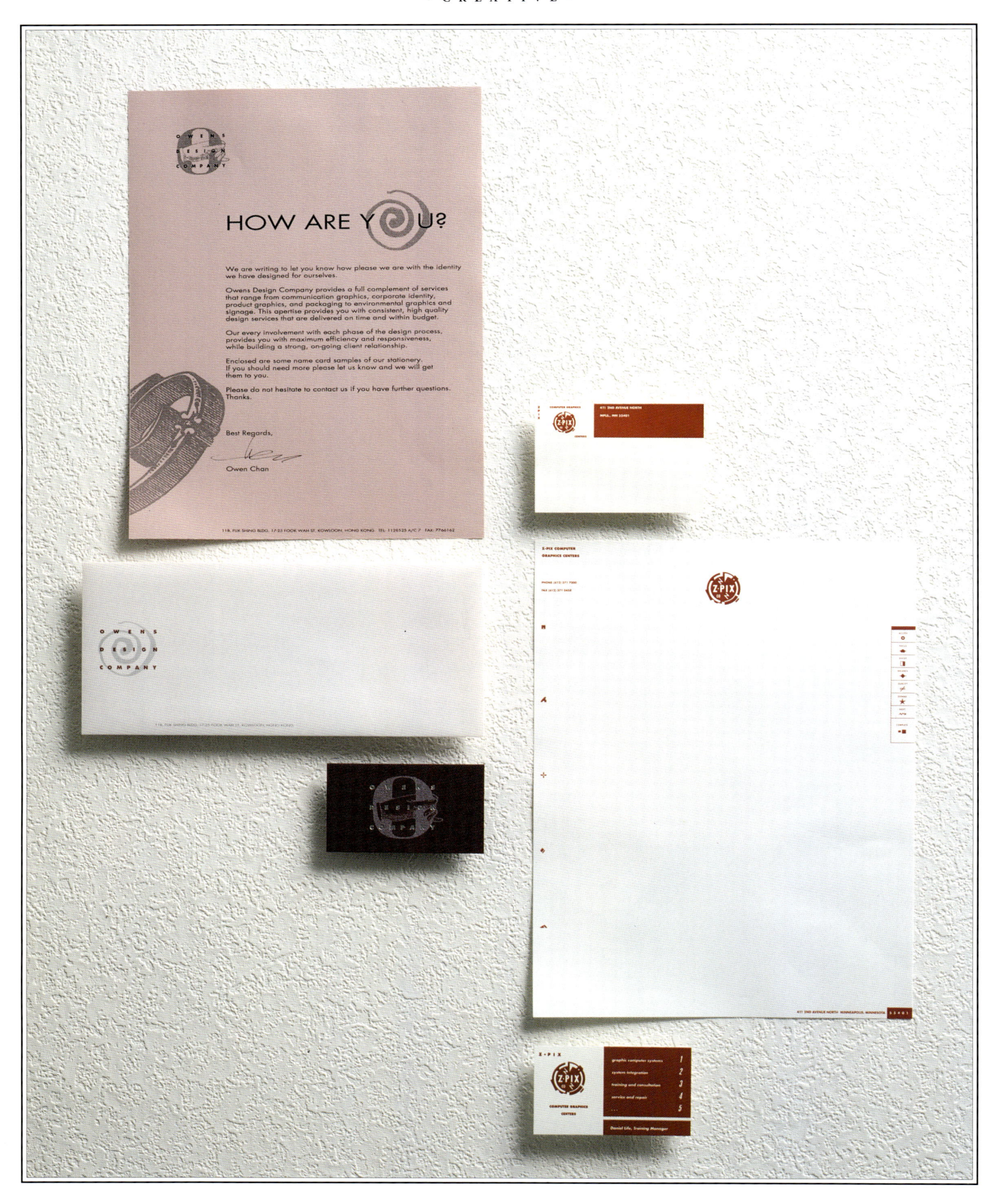

OWENS DESIGN COMPANY　Graphic Design　グラフィックデザイン　HONG KONG　1992　AD: Owen Chan　D: Frankie Chan　DF: Owens Design

Z - PIX, INC.　Computer Graphics　コンピューターグラフィックス　USA　1990　AD, D: Charles Spencer Anderson　D: Daniel Olson　DF: Charles S. Anderson Design

• CREATIVE •

SOCIETY FOR ENVIRONMENTAL GRAPHIC DESIGN　Non-profit Environmental Graphic Design Organization　非営利環境グラフィックデザイン協会　USA　1993
AD, D: Clifford Stoltze　DF: Clifford Stoltze Design
PEPE ORBEIN + ASSOCIATES　Graphic Design / Signs　グラフィックデザイン / サイン　USA　1991　AD, D, I: Pepe Orbein　DF: Pepe Orbein + Associates

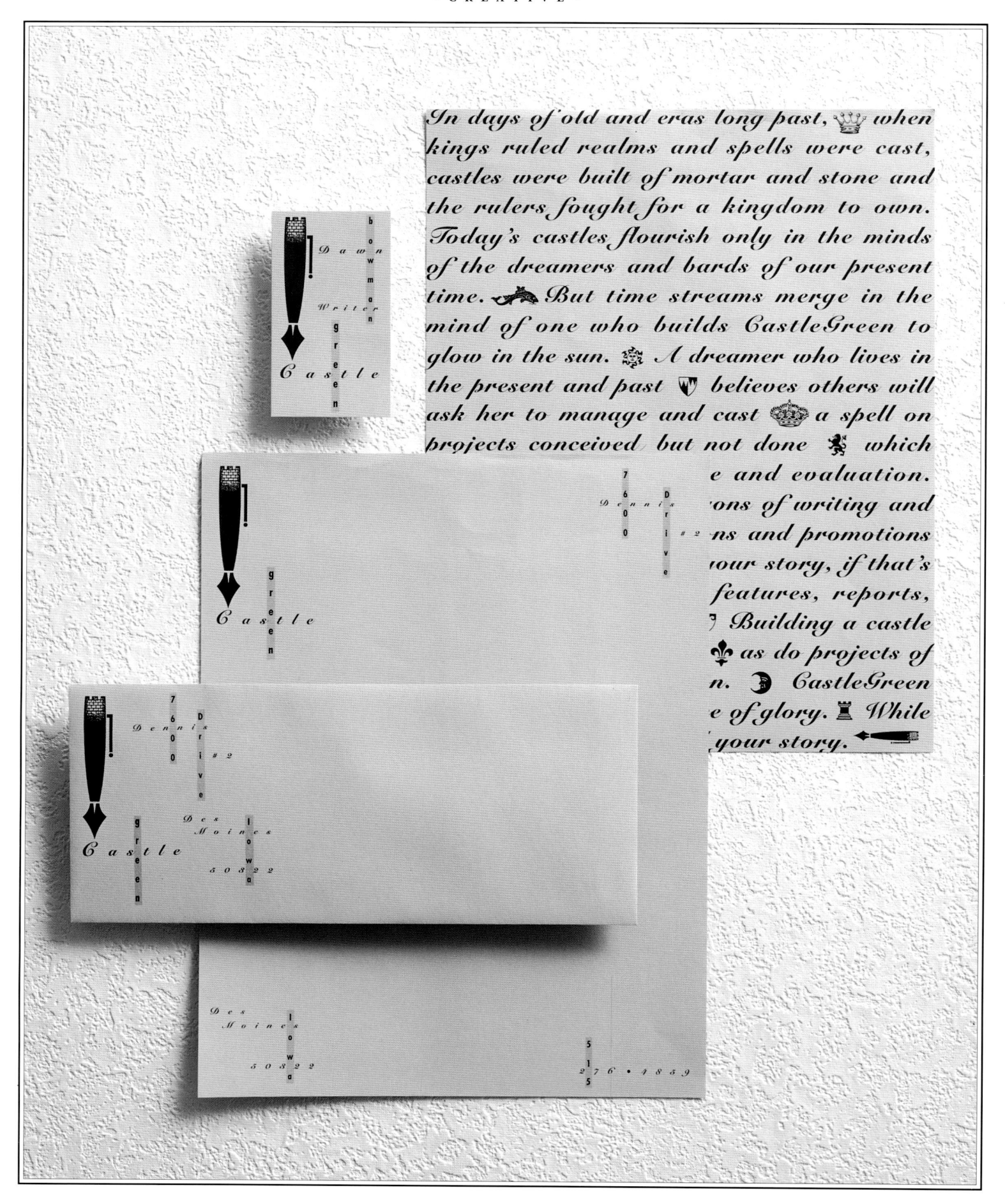

CASTLE GREEN Freelance Copywriter フリーランス・コピーライター USA 1993 AD, D, I: John Sayles CW: Dawn Bowman DF: Sayles Graphic Design

SEEGERS EN GOMBEER VORMGEVING　Graphic Design　グラフィックデザイン　BELGIUM　1992　CD, D: Wim Gombeer　AD: Marloes Seegers　DF: Seegers En Gombeer Vormgeving

• CREATIVE •

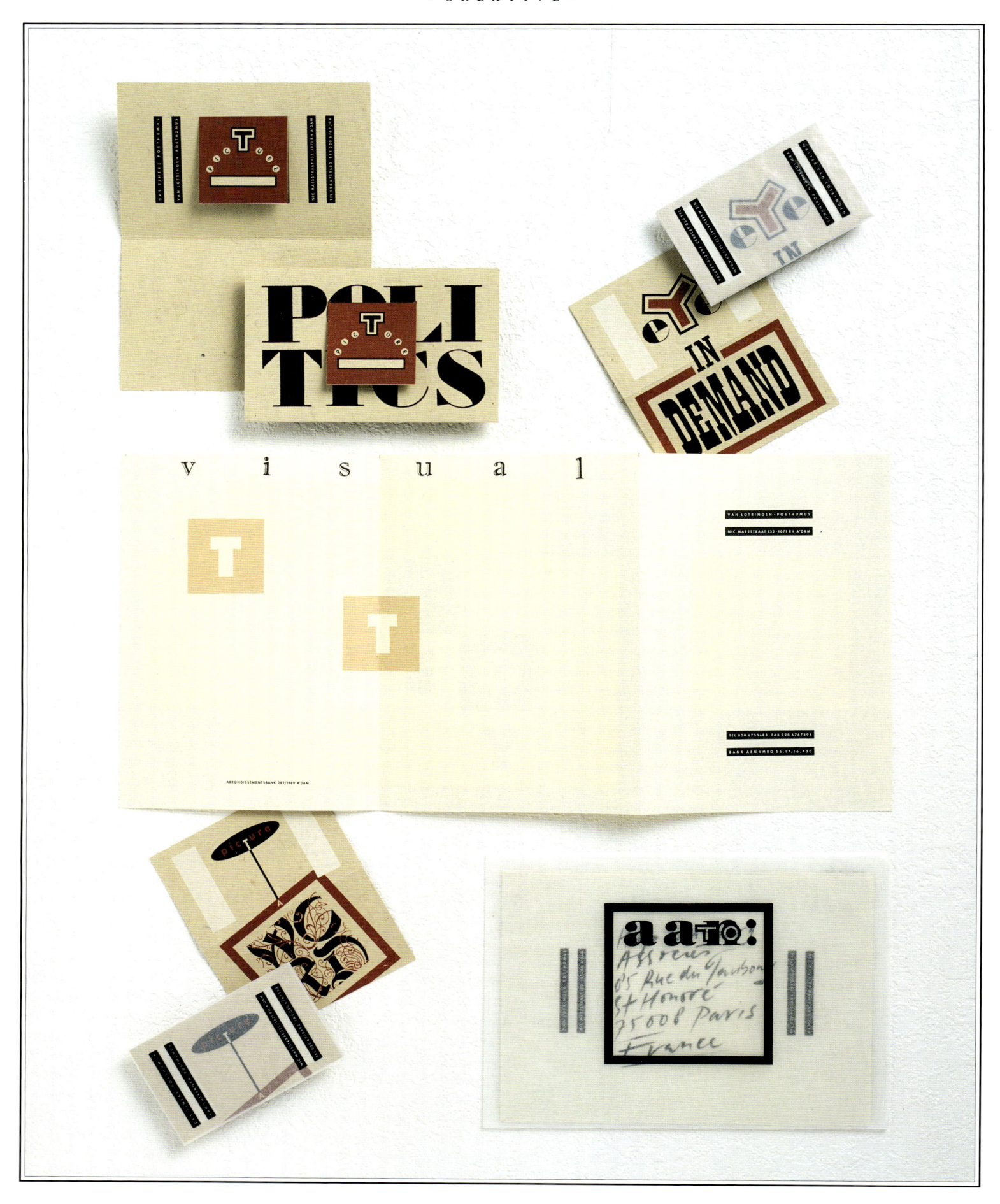

WALTER VAN LOTRINGEN / TINEKE POSTHUMUS Freelance Illustrator / Art Historian フリーランス・イラストレーター / 美術歴史学者 THE NETHERLANDS 1991
AD: Teun Anders VBAT   D: Marc Lochs   CW: Walter van Lotringen

• CREATIVE •

VANDAMME REPRESENTS   Artist   アーティスト   USA   1990   AD, D: Dannis Crowe / Neal Zimmermann   D: John Pappas   DF: Zimmermann Crowe Design

• CREATIVE •

CAVU DESIGN　Graphic Design and Marketing　グラフィックデザイン、マーケティング　USA　1993　D: Barry Kettery　DF: Cavu Design

• C R E A T I V E •

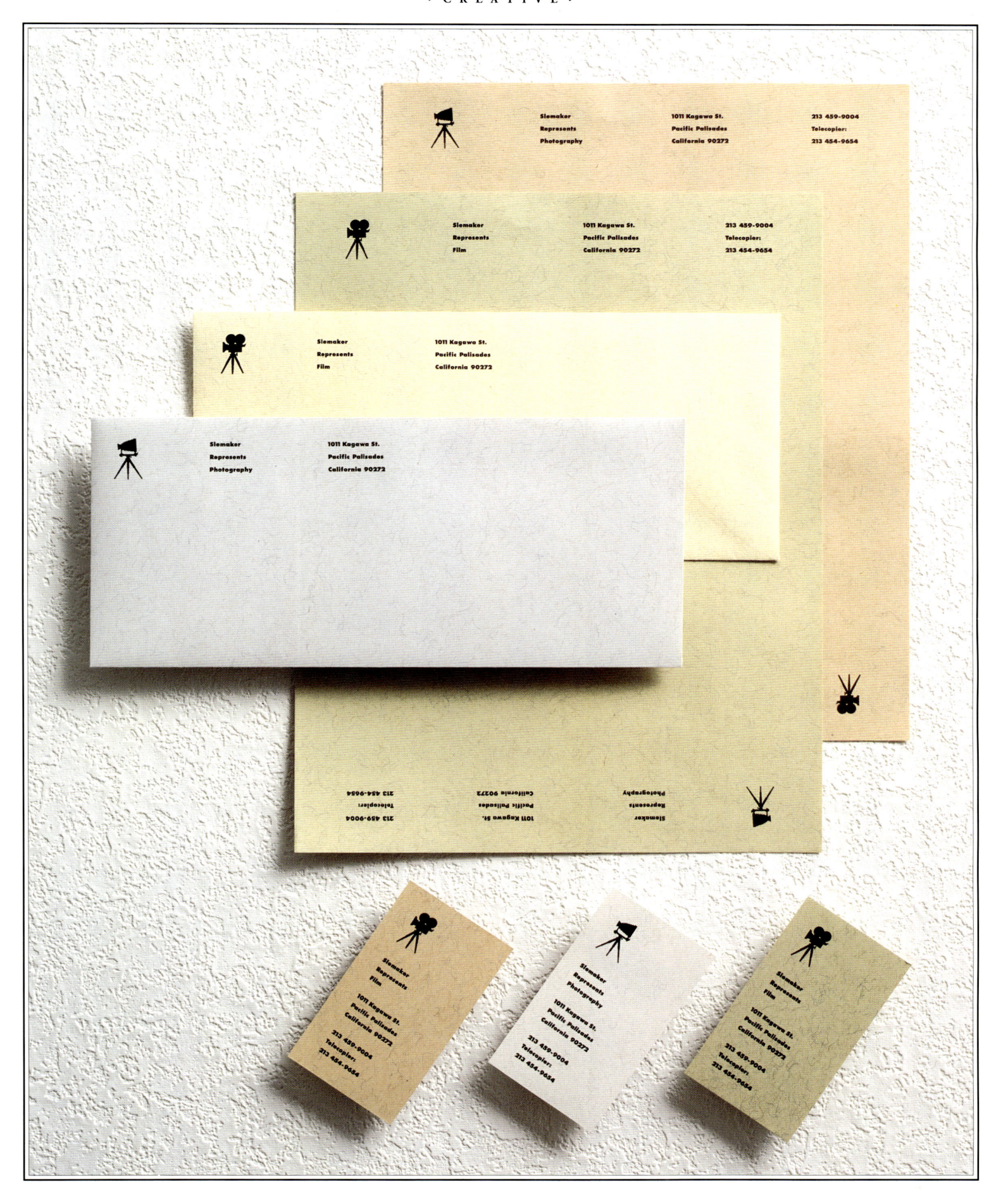

SLEMAKER REPRESENTS Photographic and Film Representative 写真、映画演出 USA 1991 AD, D, I: Joe Baratelli DF: Joseph Baratelli Design

• CREATIVE •

IFF COMPANY INC. Package Design パッケージデザイン JAPAN 1992-1993 AD: Ving Takahashi D: Masakazu Tagawa / Tomoko Masuda

• CREATIVE •

CONCEPT WORKS SHIGOTOBA INC.   Advertising and Graphic Design   広告企画・制作、CI・VI 計画   JAPAN 1991   CD: Masamori Tani   AD: Tetsuya Daimatsu   D: Asami Nakada

• CREATIVE •

KOZO TAKEUCHI Photographer 写真家 JAPAN 1992 AD, D: Yoshiro Kajitani D: Michiko Arakawa DF: Kajitani Design Room

• CREATIVE •

TASTE INC Graphic Design グラフィックデザイン JAPAN 1992 AD, D: Toshiyasu Nanbu

• C R E A T I V E •

GULLIVER CO., LTD. Printing プリンティング JAPAN 1992 CD: Seiji Koseki AD: Tatsuomi Majima D: 1. Takashi Nomura / 2. Koichi Sato / 3. Yoichirou Fujii / 4. Masatoshi Toda

• CREATIVE •

GULLIVER CO., LTD. Printing プリンティング JAPAN 1992 CD: Seiji Koseki AD: Tatsuomi Majima D: 1. Teruhiko Yumura / 2. Nobuo Nakagaki / 3. Keisuke Konishi / 4. Yukimasa Okumura

• CREATIVE •

KOWALSKI DESIGNWORKS, INC.　Graphic Design　グラフィックデザイン　USA 1991　AD: Stephen Kowalski　D: Janél Apple　P: George Post　DF: Kowalski Designworks

• CREATIVE •

DESIGN LABORATORY Graphic Design   グラフィックデザイン   JAPAN 1992   AD, D: Tsuyokatsu Kudo   P: Satoru Ebina   DF: Design Laboratory

• C R E A T I V E •

HUNDRED INC. Graphic Design グラフィックデザイン JAPAN 1992 AD, D: Yuko Araki DF: Hundred

• CREATIVE •

TSUYOKATSU KUDO Graphic Design グラフィックデザイン JAPAN 1992 AD, D: Tsuyokatsu Kudo P: Satoru Ebina DF: Design Laboratory

• CREATIVE •

GENQUI NUMATA   Artist   芸術家   JAPAN   1990 - 1993   ARTIST: Genqui Numata

• CREATIVE •

JOHN SPOSATO DESIGN + ILLUSTRATION Graphic Design グラフィックデザイン USA 1989 D, I: John Sposato

• CREATIVE •

BRADFORD LAWTON DESIGN GROUP　Graphic Design　グラフィックデザイン　USA 1992
CD, D, I: Bradford Lawton　AD, D, I: Jody Laney　AD: Jennifer Griffith Garcia　DF: The Bradford Lawton Design Group

• CREATIVE •

MODERN DOG Graphic Design グラフィックデザイン USA 1993 AD, D, I: Robynne Raye D: Michael Strassburger DF: Modern Dog

• C R E A T I V E •

MODERN DOG Graphic Design グラフィックデザイン USA 1993 AD, D, CW: Michael Strassburger DF: Modern Dog

• MEDIA / COMMUNICATIONS •

KEES KASANDER   Film, Television and Theater Production   映画、TV、劇の制作   THE NETHERLANDS   1990   AD, D, I: Ruud van Empel   DF: Ruud van Empel

CHUCKIE-BOY RECORDS   Record Co.   レコード会社   USA   1990   AD, D, P: Art Chantry   I: Peter Bagge   DF: Art Chantry

• MEDIA / COMMUNICATIONS •

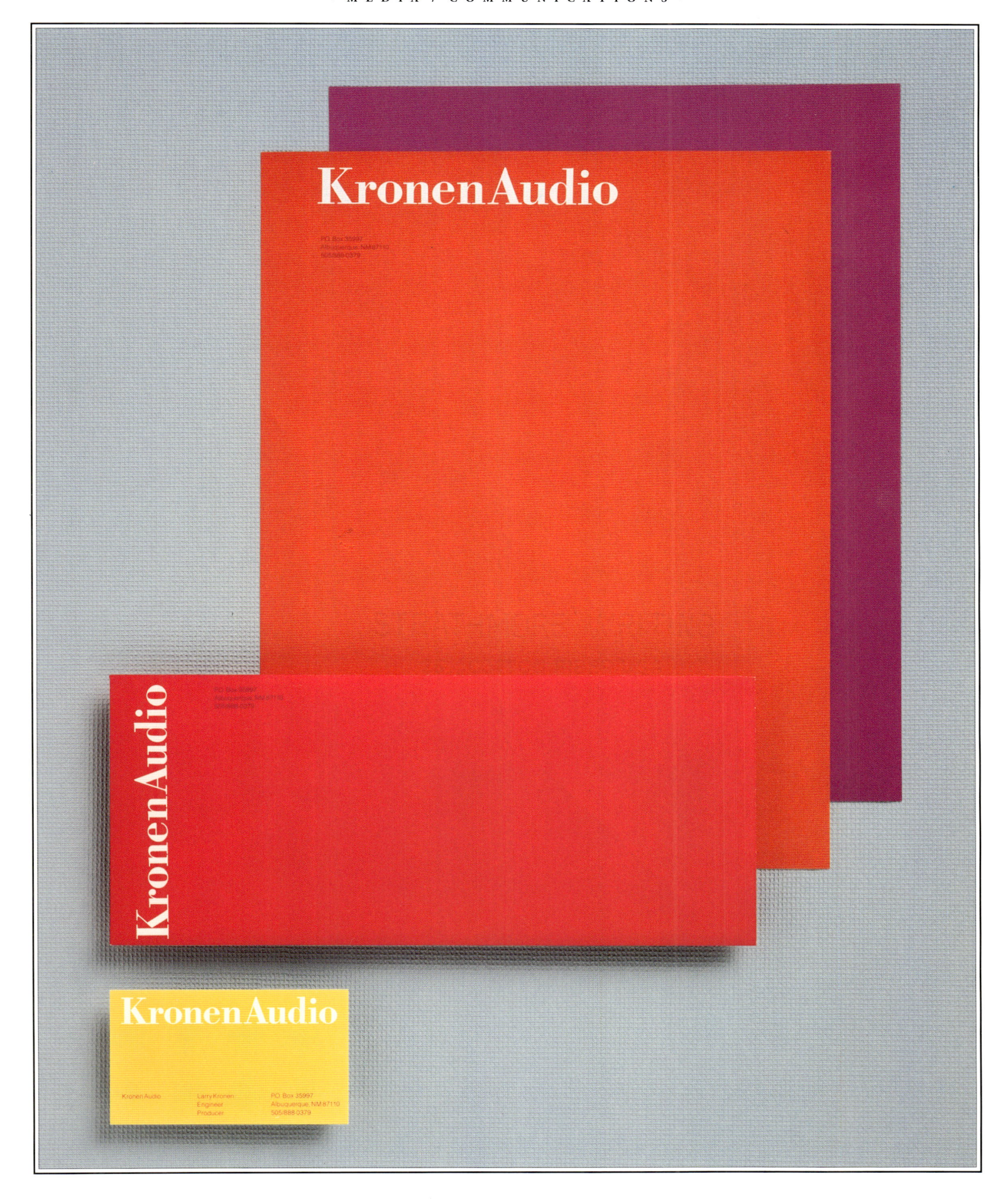

KRONEN AUDIO　Audio Engineering and Production　オーディオ技工、製作　USA　1988　AD, D: Steve Wedeen　DF: Vaughn Wedeen Creative

• MEDIA / COMMUNICATIONS •

LA 4ÈME DIMENSION   Communication Agency   通信機関   FRANCE 1991   AD, D: Jean-Jacques Tachdjian   DF: I Comme Image

• MEDIA / COMMUNICATIONS •

ACACIA AGENCY Magazine Agency 雑誌取次 FRANCE 1991 AD, D: Jean-Jacques Tachdjian DF: I Comme Image

• M E D I A   /   C O M M U N I C A T I O N S •

SANWOOD STUDIO Music Studio, Music Publisher and Label ミュージックレーベル、スタジオ、出版 GERMANY 1990 CD: Matthias Simon AD, D, I: Rudiger Gotz DF: Stubenrauch + Simon
AUDIO VISUAL ENTERPRISE CENTRE Center for Cultural Industries 文化産業センター UK 1990 AD, D: The Designers Republic DF: The Designers Republic
SHEFFIELD CITY COUNCIL'S RED TAPE STUDIOS Recording and Rehearsal Studios レコーディング、リハーサルスタジオ UK 1990 AD, D: The Designers Republic DF: The Designers Republic

• MEDIA / COMMUNICATIONS •

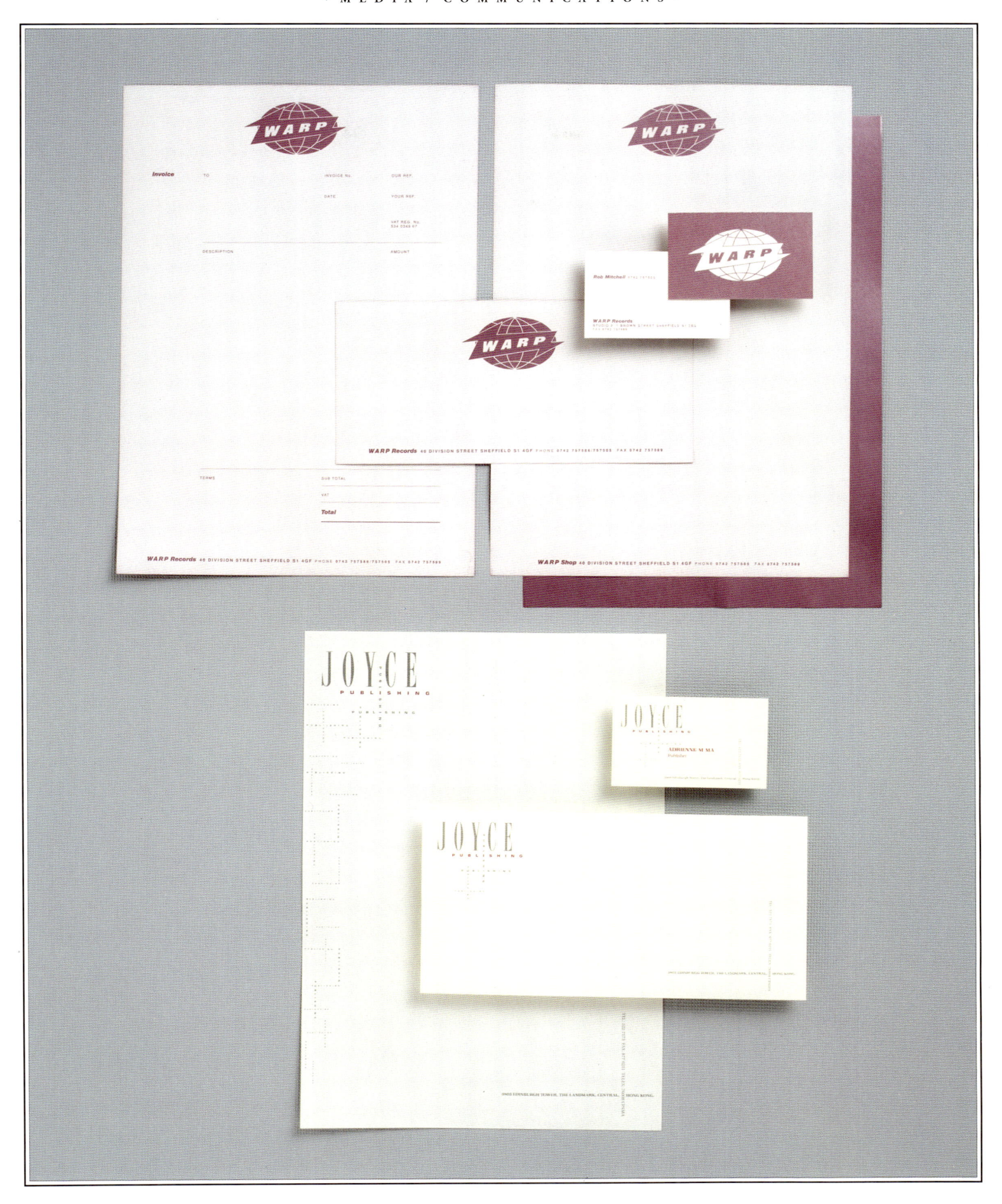

WARP RECORDS Record Label and Music Shop レコードレーベル、販売 UK 1991 AD, D: The Designers Republic DF: The Designers Republic

JOYCE PUBLISHING Publishing 出版 HONG KONG 1991 AD, D: Alan Chan D: Chen Shun Tsoi DF: Alan Chan Design

• MEDIA / COMMUNICATIONS •

MCGUIRE WILHOITE   Communications Service   通信サービス   USA 1992   CD: Patrick McGuire / Melanie Wilhoite   AD, D: Vittorio Costarella   DF: Modern Dog

• MEDIA / COMMUNICATIONS •

RADIO VISION INTERNATIONAL　Film Production　映画制作　USA　1991　D: Margo Chase　DF: Margo Chase Design

• MEDIA / COMMUNICATIONS •

THE WATER COMPANY Music Publisher 音楽出版 THE NETHERLANDS 1990 AD, D: Anton Vos DF: Dedato

• MEDIA / COMMUNICATIONS •

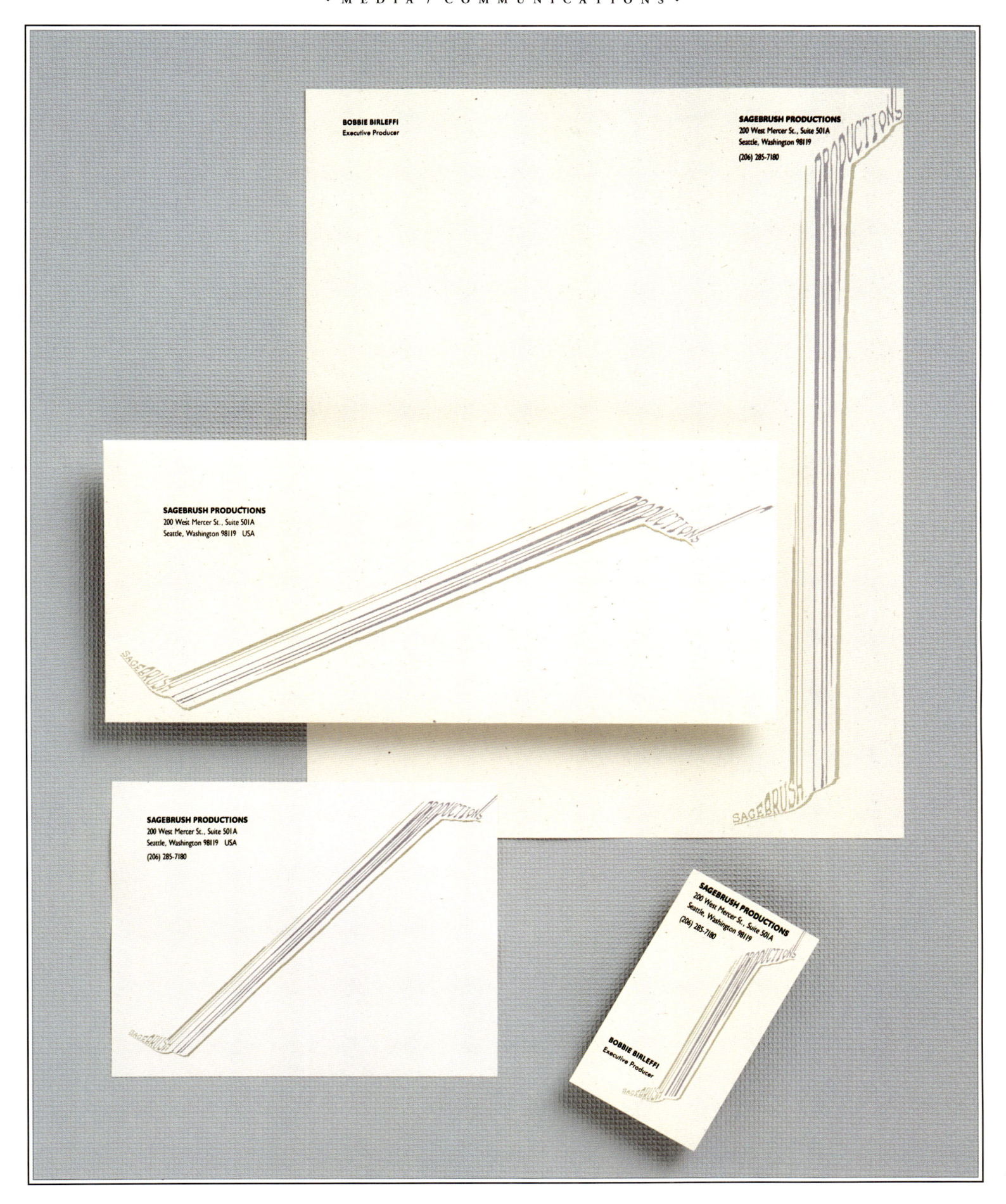

SAGEBRUSH PRODUCTIONS Independent Art Film Production 映画制作 USA 1991 AD, D, P, I, CW: Art Chantry Design DF: Art Chantry Design

• MEDIA / COMMUNICATIONS •

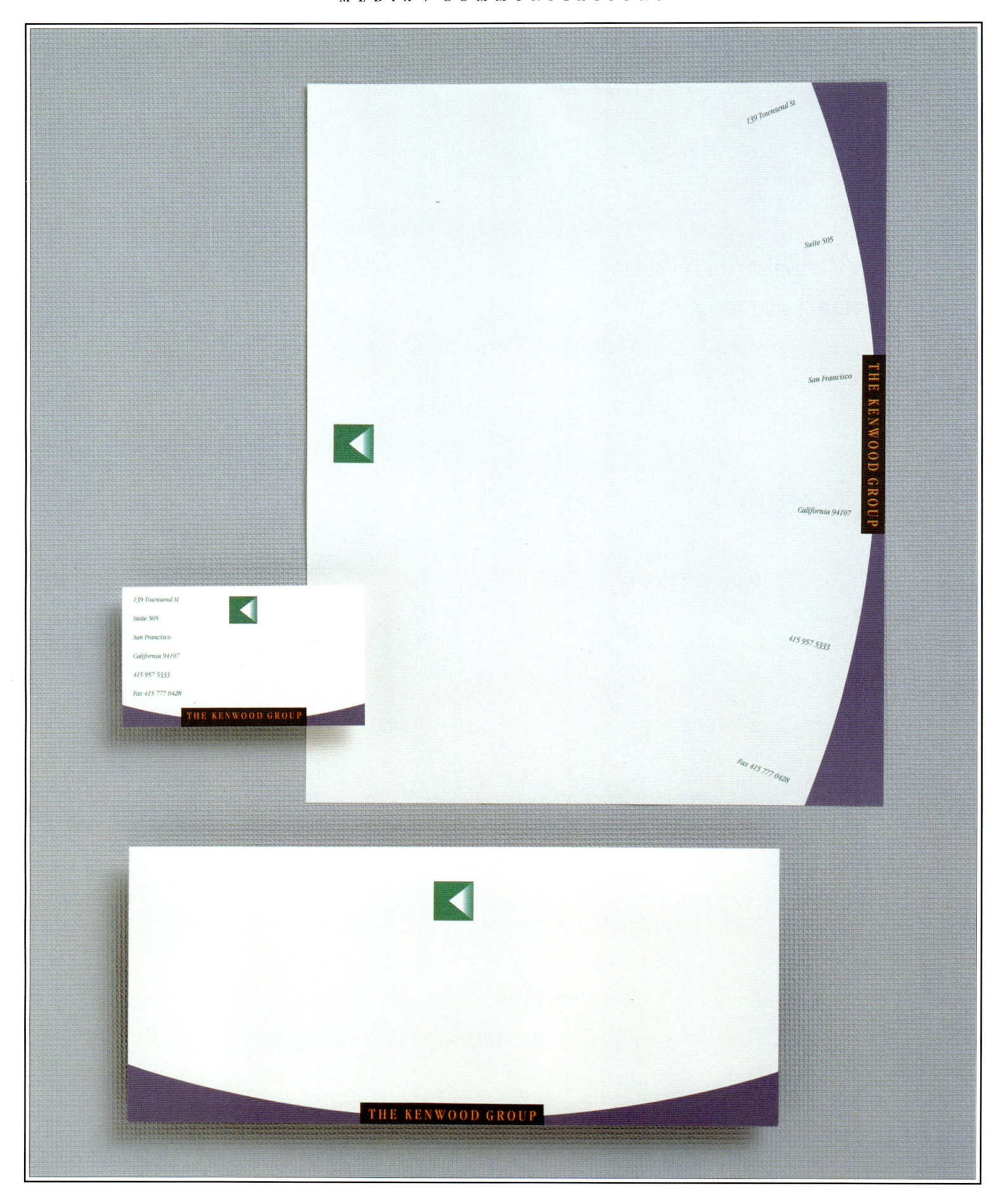

THE KENWOOD GROUP   Communications (Film, Video, Multimedia, Meetings & Events)   メディア、イベント情報通信   USA   1992
AD, D: Hock Wah Yeo   D: Cary Chiao   DF: The Design Office of Wong & Yeo

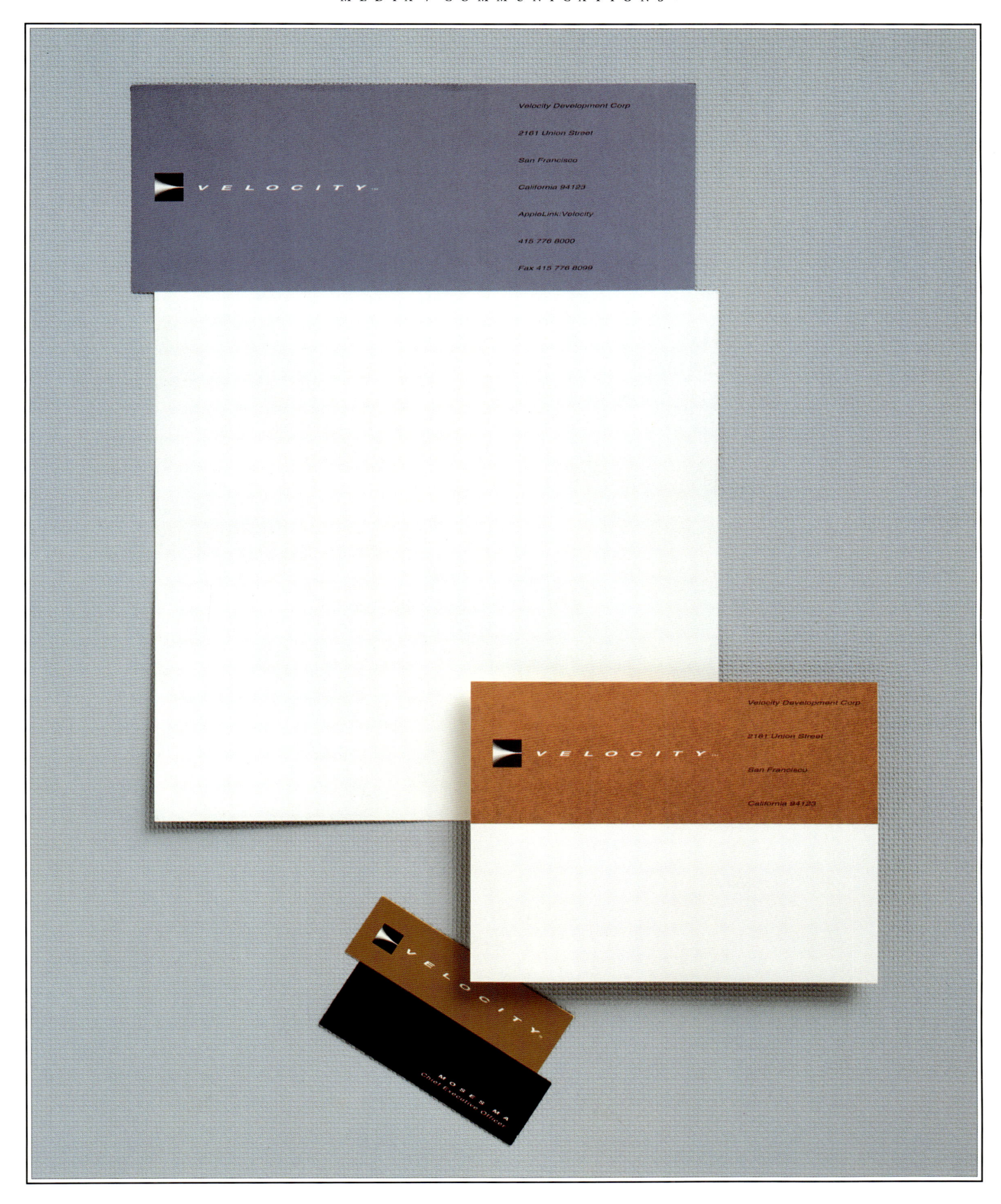

• MEDIA / COMMUNICATIONS •

VELOCITY DEVELOPMENT CORPORATION Computer Software Publishers コンピューターソフトウェア発行 USA 1991
AD, D, I: Hock Wah Yeo   D: Cary Chiao   DF: The Design Office of Wong & Yeo

• MEDIA / COMMUNICATIONS •

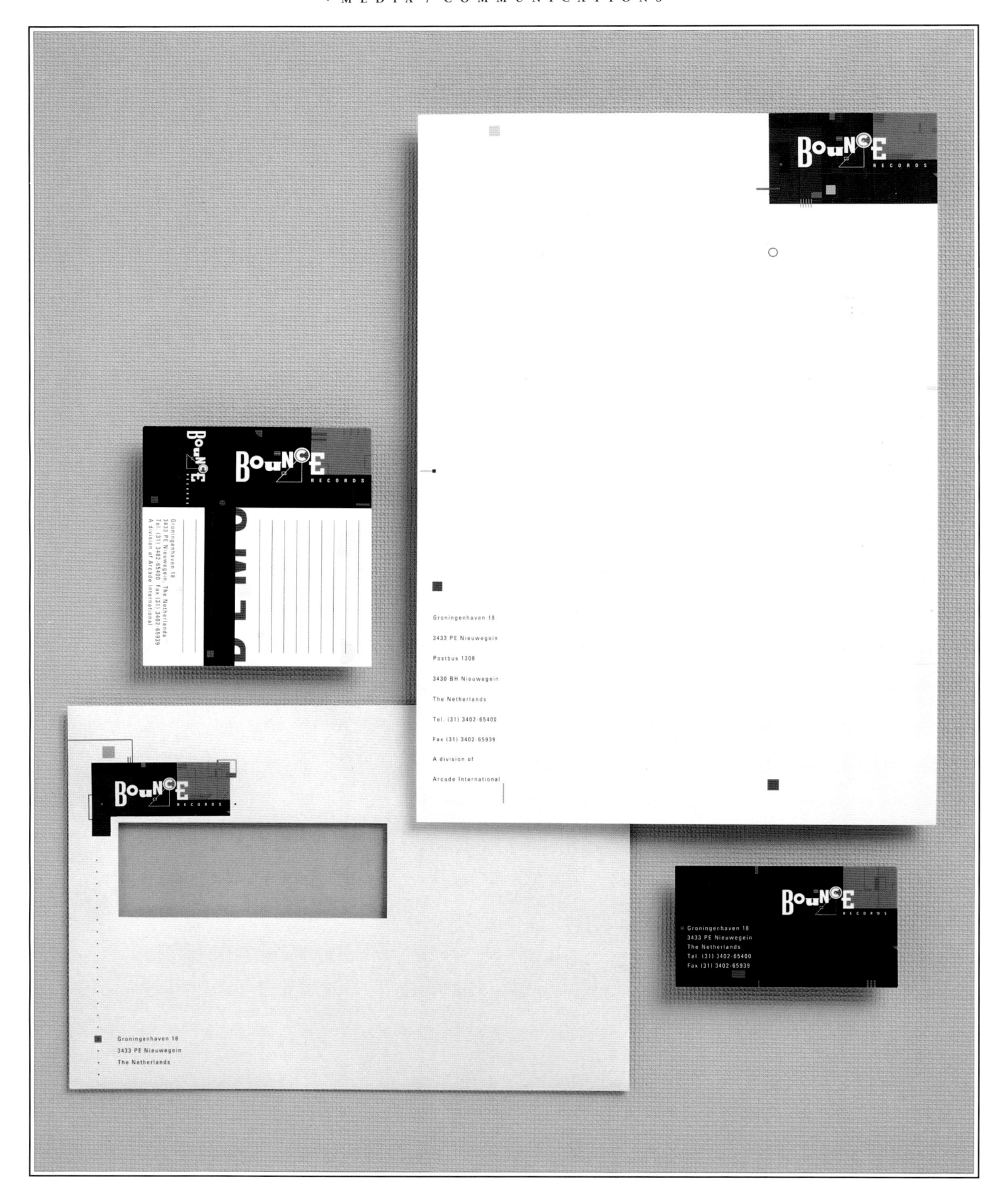

BOUNCE RECORDS   Record Company   レコード会社   THE NETHERLANDS 1990 AD, D: Anton Vos   D: Marute Wigger   DF: Dedato

• M E D I A   /   C O M M U N I C A T I O N S •

SOFTWARE TOO CORPORATION   Computer Related Service   コンピューター関連ソフト・ハードウェアの輸入、販売、代理業   JAPAN 1991
AD: Naomi Enami   D: Mariko Yamamoto   DF: Propeller Art Works

PRU REX - HASSAN   Film Production   映画制作   UK 1990   AD, D: Teresa Roviras   DF: Teresa Roviras

• MEDIA / COMMUNICATIONS •

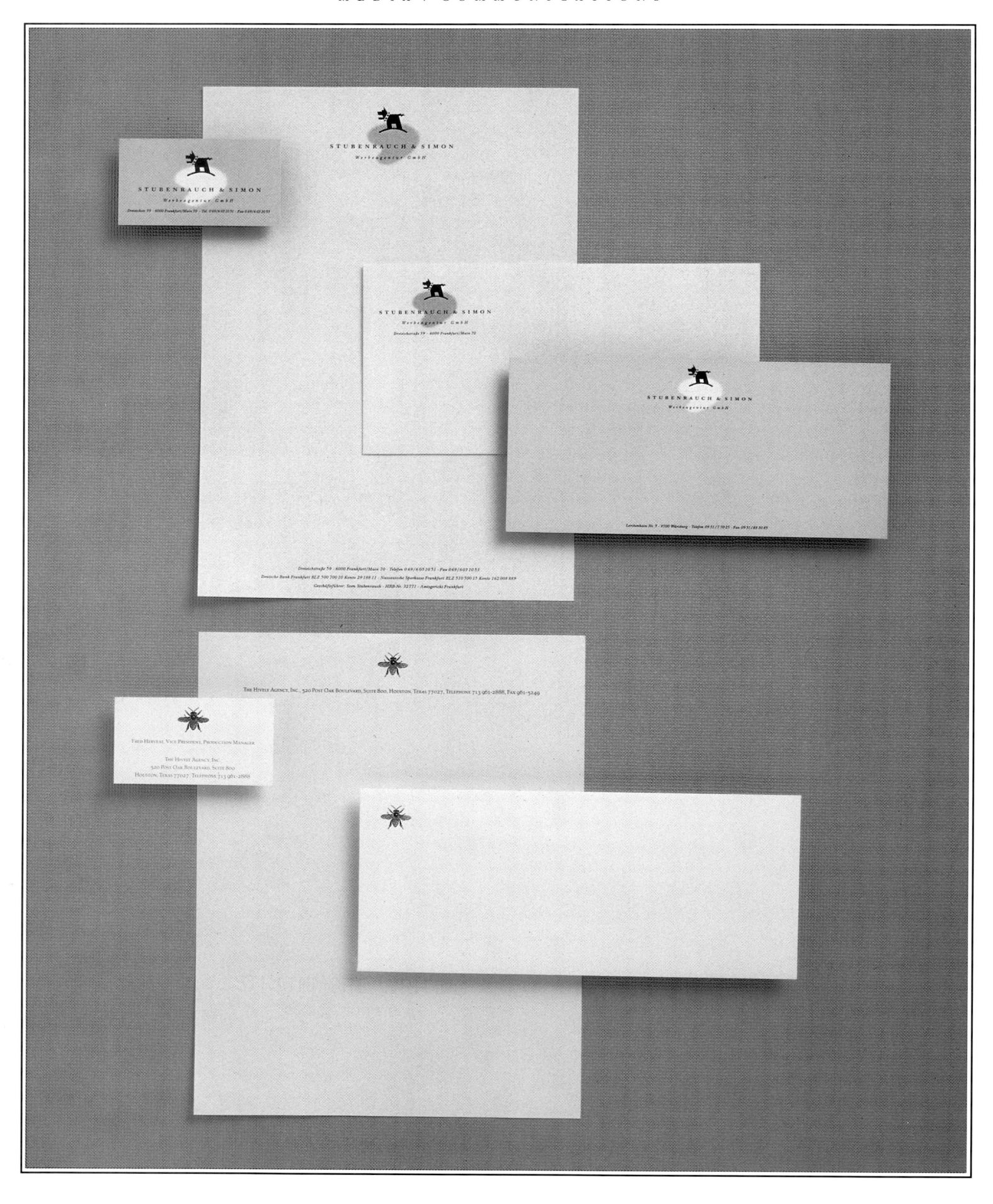

STUBENRAUCH + SIMON Advertising Agency 広告代理店 GERMANY 1991 CD: Matthias Simon AD, D, I: Rudiger Gotz DF: Stubenrauch + Simon
THE HIVELY AGENCY Advertising Agency 広告代理店 USA 1985 AD, D, CW: Charles Hively I: Bettman Archives

• MEDIA / COMMUNICATIONS •

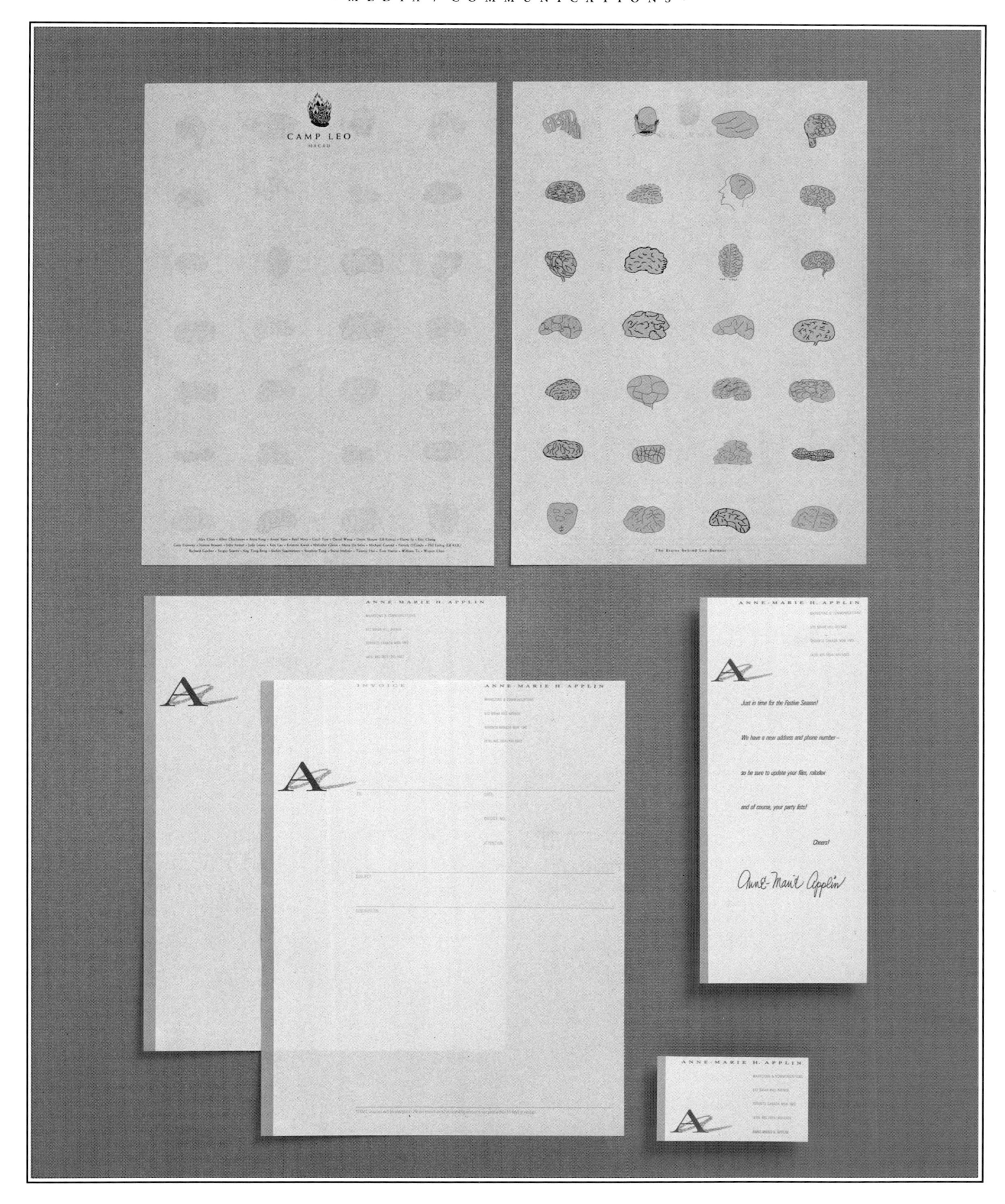

LEO BURNETT   Advertising Agency   広告代理店   HONG KONG   1991   CD: Gary Conway   AD: Stefan Sagmeister   D: Peter Rae   I: Mike Chan   DF: Leo Burnett Design Group
ANNE-MARIE APPLIN   Marketing and Communications   マーケティング、通信サービス   USA   1989   CD: Paul Browning   DF: Taylor & Browning Design Associates

• MEDIA / COMMUNICATIONS •

PRIME PUBLISHING CO. Publishing of Buddist Books 仏教本の出版 HONG KONG 1992 AD, D: Freeman Lau Siu Hong DF: Kan Tai-keung Design & Associates

• MEDIA / COMMUNICATIONS •

FIELD AND WALL PRODUCTIONS, INC. Television Commercial Productions   テレビコマーシャル制作   USA 1989 AD, D: Peter Bradford   I: Joyce Rothschild   DF: Peter Bradford and Associates

• MEDIA / COMMUNICATIONS •

BLIND SPOT, INC.   Photography Magazine   写真雑誌   USA   1993   CD: Robert Bergman-ungar   D: Liong The

• MEDIA / COMMUNICATIONS •

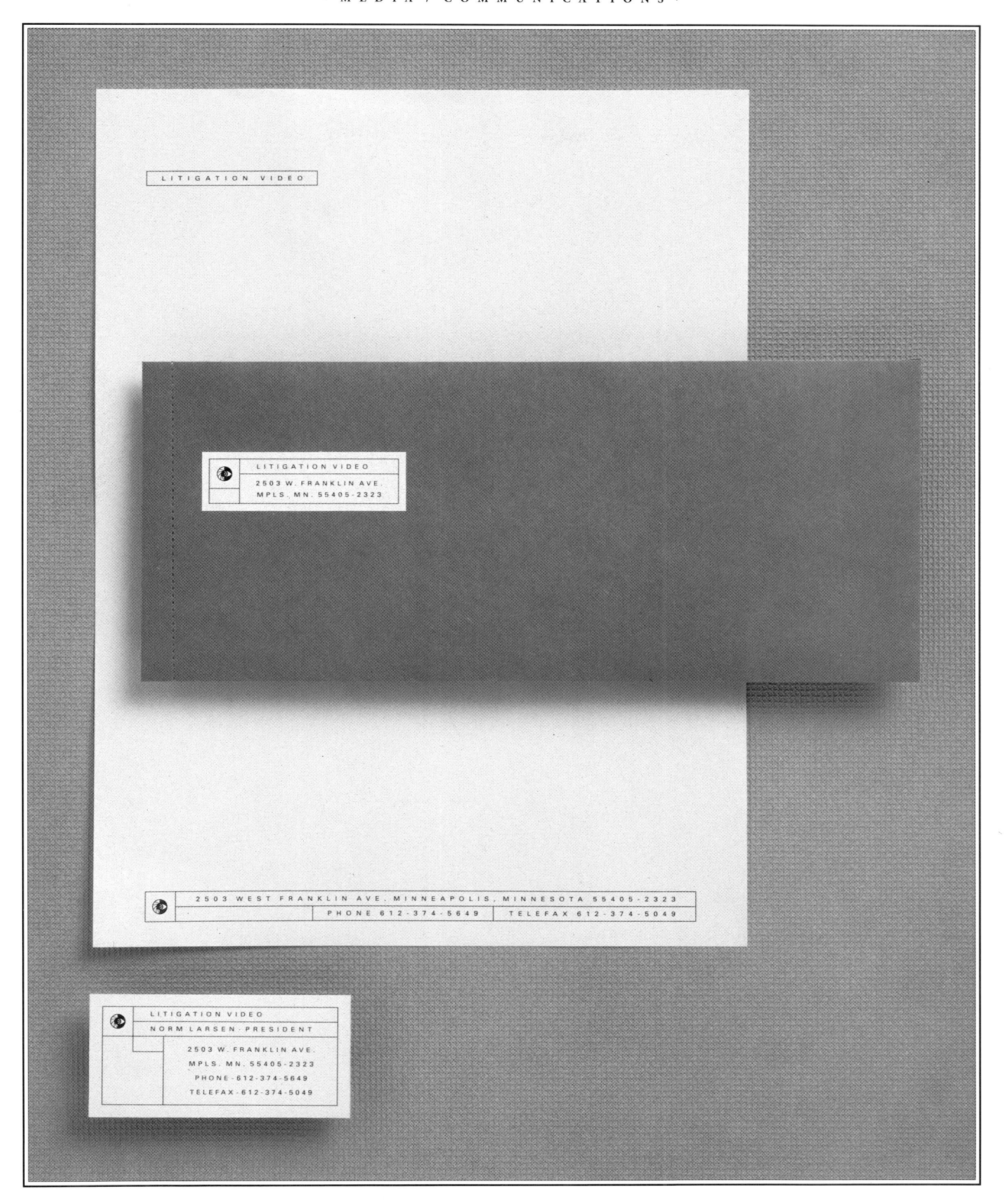

LITIGATION VIDEO (NORM LARSEN, PRES.) Legal Videos 法定のビデオ会社 USA 1992 AD, D: Todd Hauswirth AD: Daniel Olson DF: Charles S. Anderson Design

• MEDIA / COMMUNICATIONS •

MOMENTUM FILMS Commercial and Film Production Company コマーシャル、映画制作 USA 1988
CD: Forrest Richardson   CD, AD: Varerie Richardson   D: Jim Bolek   DF: Richardson or Richardson

• MEDIA / COMMUNICATIONS •

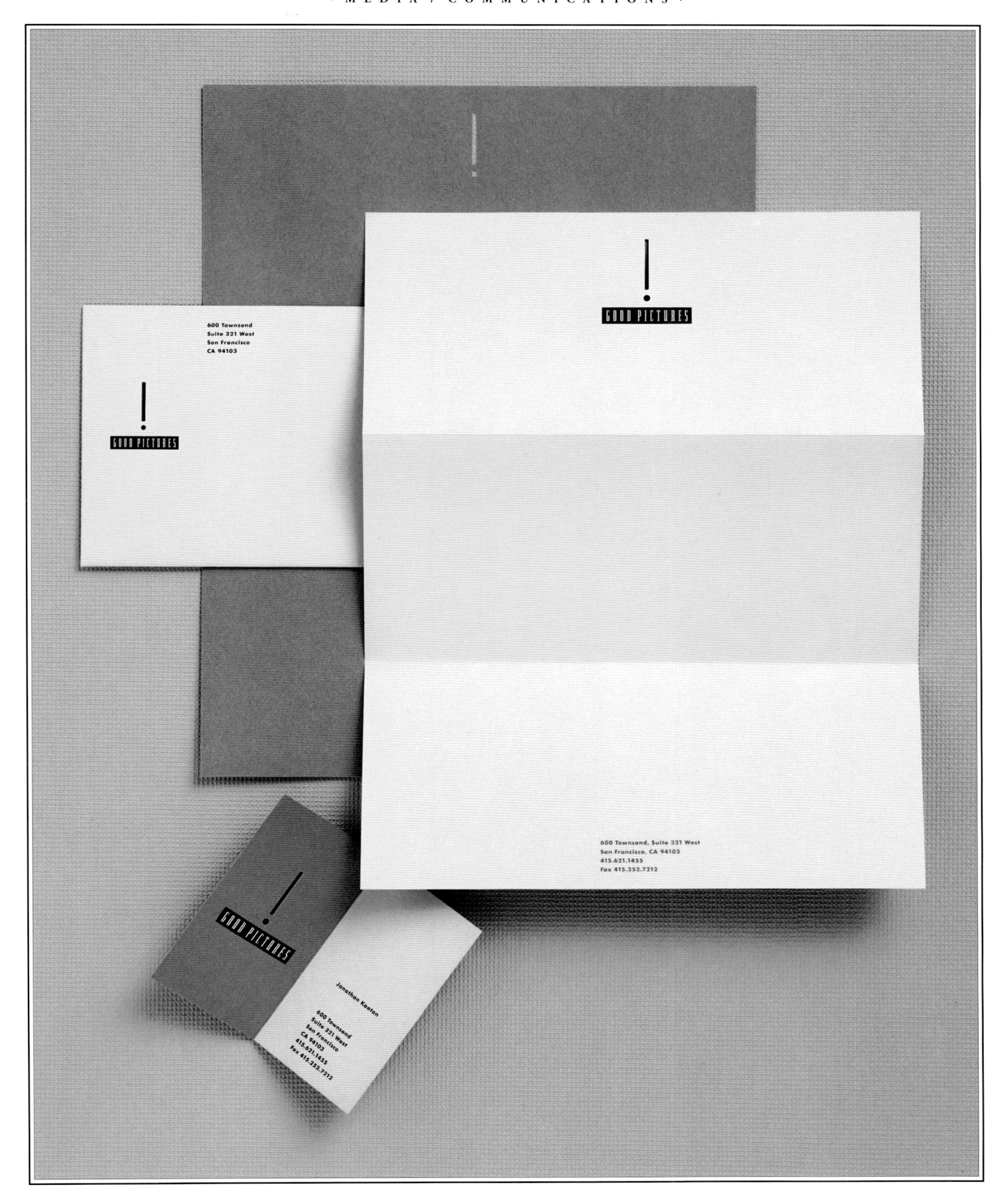

GOOD PICTURES Video Production Facility ビデオ制作 USA 1991 AD, D: Jennifer Morla D: Sharrie Brooks

• RETAIL / COMMERCE •

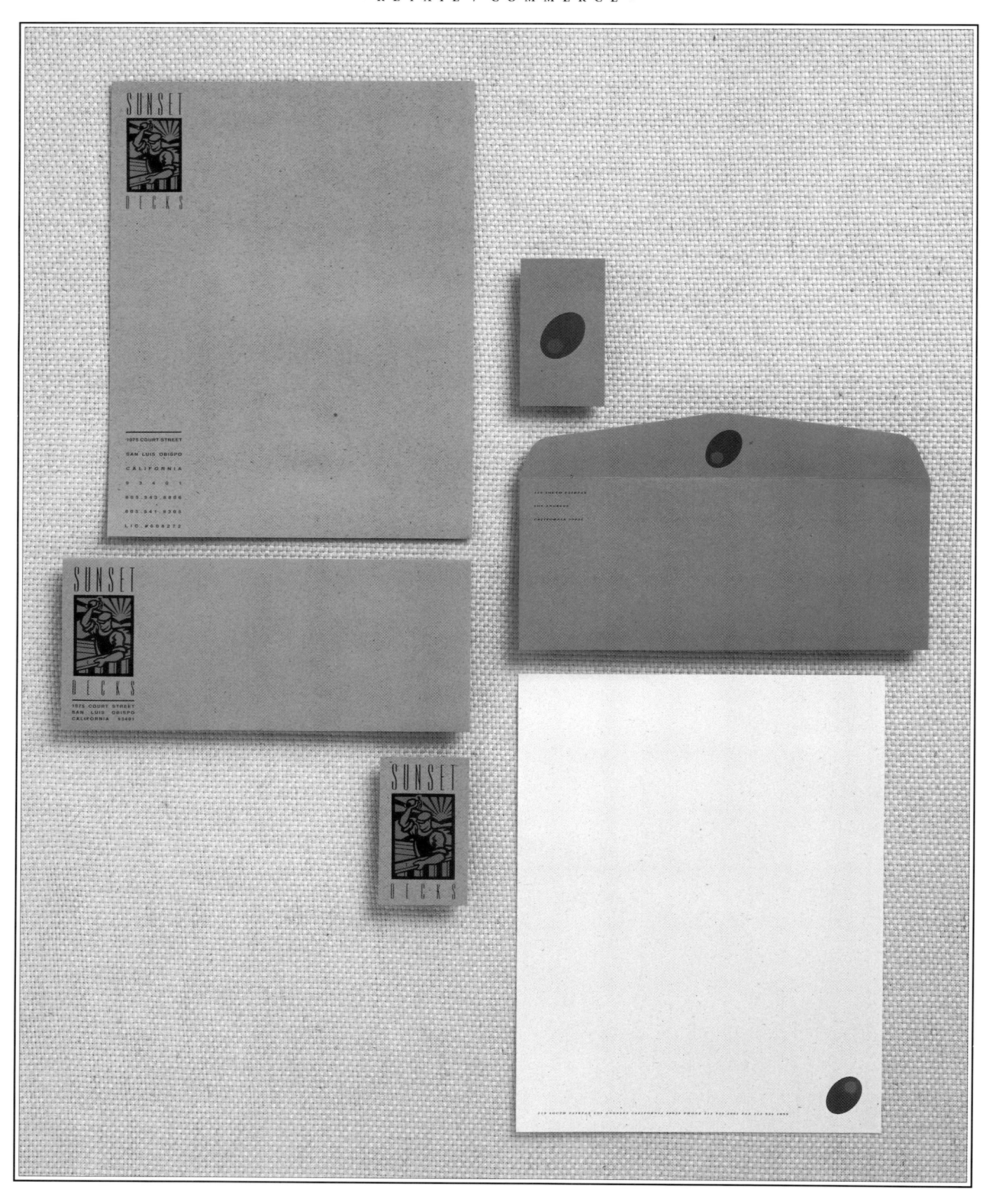

SUNSET DECKS Custom Design and Crafts 受注デザイン、手工芸 USA 1991 AD: Stephen Kowalski D: Janél Apple I: Camille Sauvé DF: Kowalski Design Works

THE OLIVE Restaurant レストラン USA 1990 CD: Richard Seireeni D: Romane Cameron DF: Studio Seireeni

• RETAIL / COMMERCE •

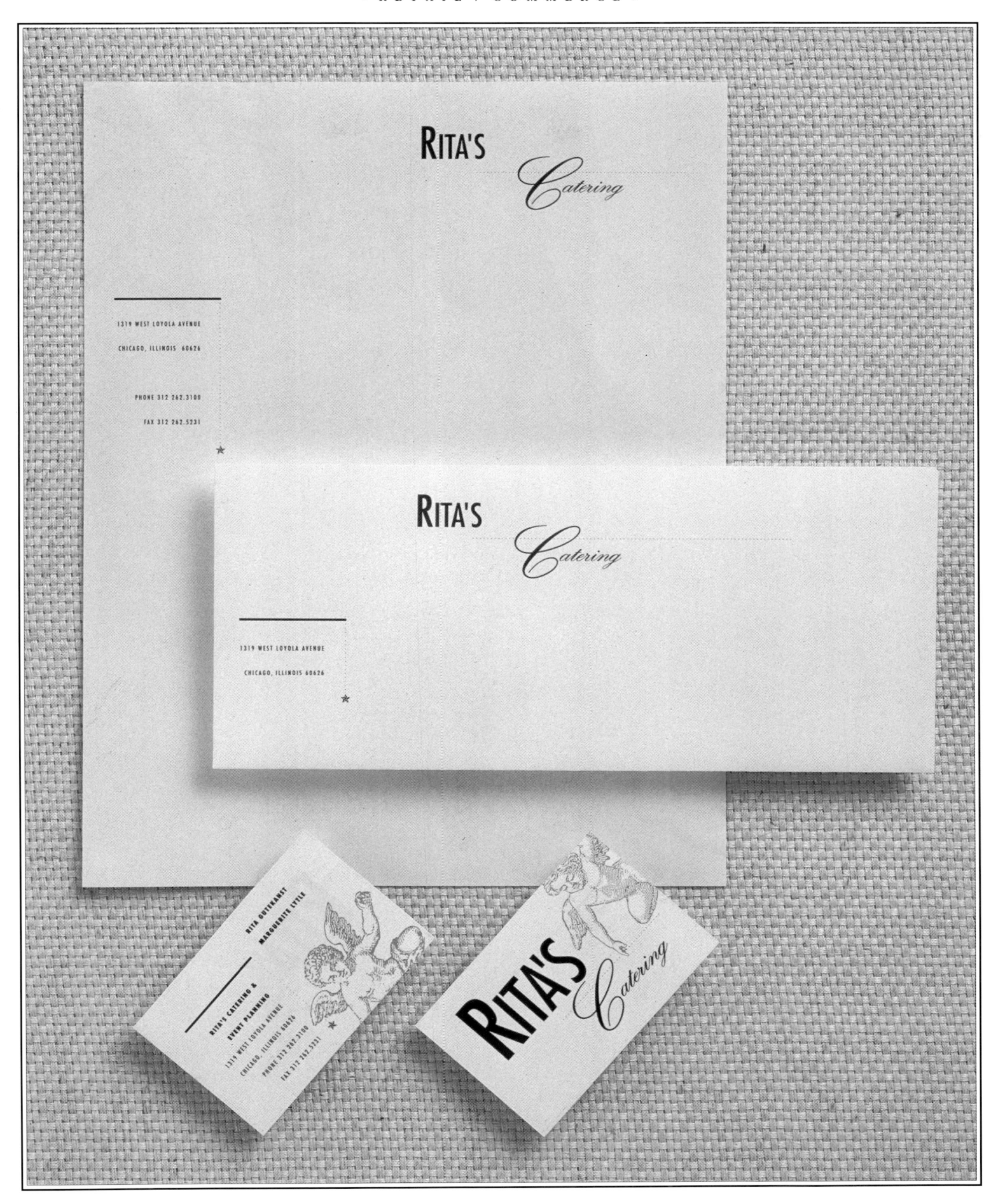

RITA'S CATERING Catering 料理調達 USA 1990 AD, D: Mark Oldach DF: Mark Oldach Design

• RETAIL / COMMERCE •

OBUNSHA PACIFIC CORPORATION   Tea House   喫茶店   HONG KONG   1991   AD, D: Alan Chan   D: Phillip Leung   DF: Alan Chan Design

• 116 •

• RETAIL / COMMERCE •

D. D. II KARAOKE　Karaoke Lounge　カラオケラウンジ　HONG KONG　1990　AD, D: Alan Chan　D: Alvin Chan　DF: Alan Chan Design
Special Effects: Metallic inks has been used for the logo and illustration.　ロゴとイラストにメタリック・インクを使用。

• RETAIL / COMMERCE •

SMASH BOX Rental Photo Studio 貸撮影室 USA 1990 D: Margo Chase DF: Margo Chase Design
STREAMLINE GRAPHICS Pre-press Service Bureau 予約サービス所 USA 1991 AD: Stan Evenson D: Glenn Sakamoto

◆ RETAIL / COMMERCE ◆

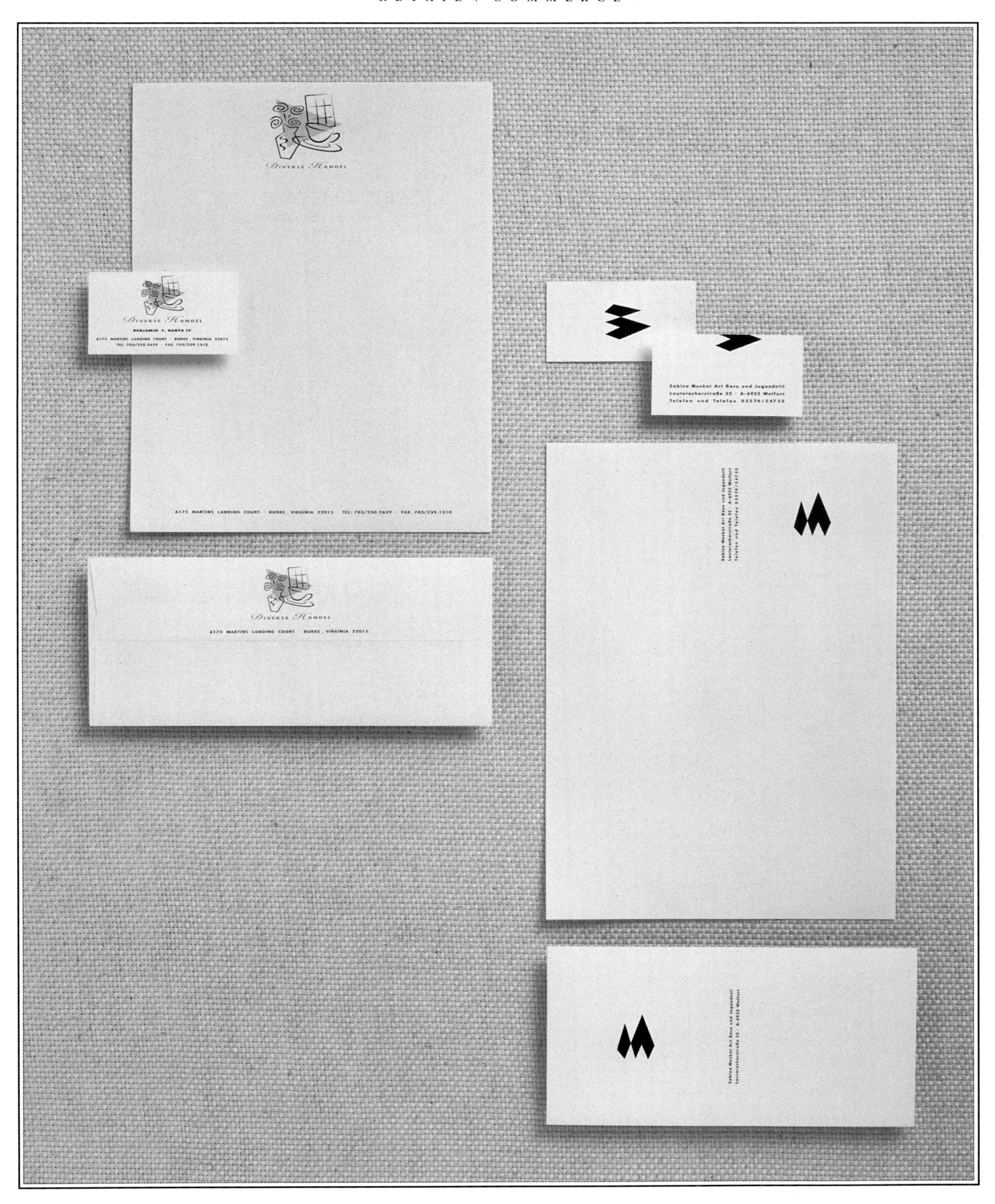

DIVERSE HANDEL　Swedish Gift Shop　スウェーデンのギフトショップ　USA　1993　AD: Supon Phornirunlit　D, I: Richard Lee Heffner　DF: Supon Design Group

SABINE MOSKAT　Art Deco Antique Furniture and Art　アールデコの家具、調度品　AUSTRIA　1991　D: Kurt Dornig　DF: Dornig Grafik Design

• RETAIL / COMMERCE •

VIANSA WINERY   Winery   ワイン醸造所   USA   1992   AD, D: Patti Britton   CALLIGRAPHER: Georgia Deaver   DF: Britton Design

◆ RETAIL / COMMERCE ◆

STREAMLINE CORPORATE PLANNERS　Travel Consultants　旅行相談所　USA　1991　AD: Michael Dunlavey　D: Heidi Tomlinson　DF: The Dunlavey Studio

• RETAIL / COMMERCE •

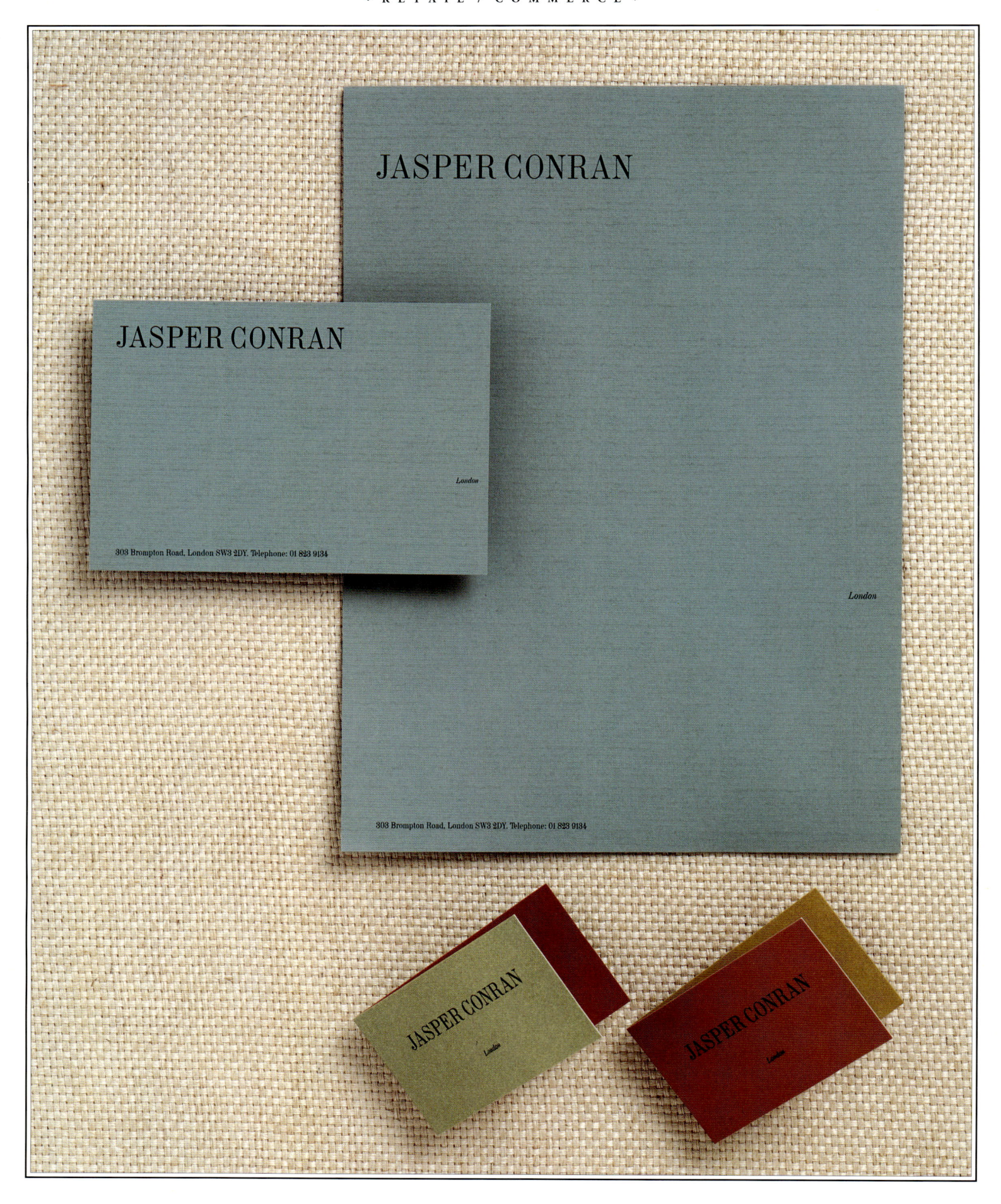

JASPER CONRAN Clothing Design ファッションデザイン UK 1990 D: Stephanie Nash / Anthony Michael DF: Michael Nash Associates

• RETAIL / COMMERCE •

VINA VALORIA CELLAR Traditional Wine Cellar ワインセラー SPAIN 1991 D: Carmen Peña DF: Carmen Peña / Provenio Design Studio

• RETAIL / COMMERCE •

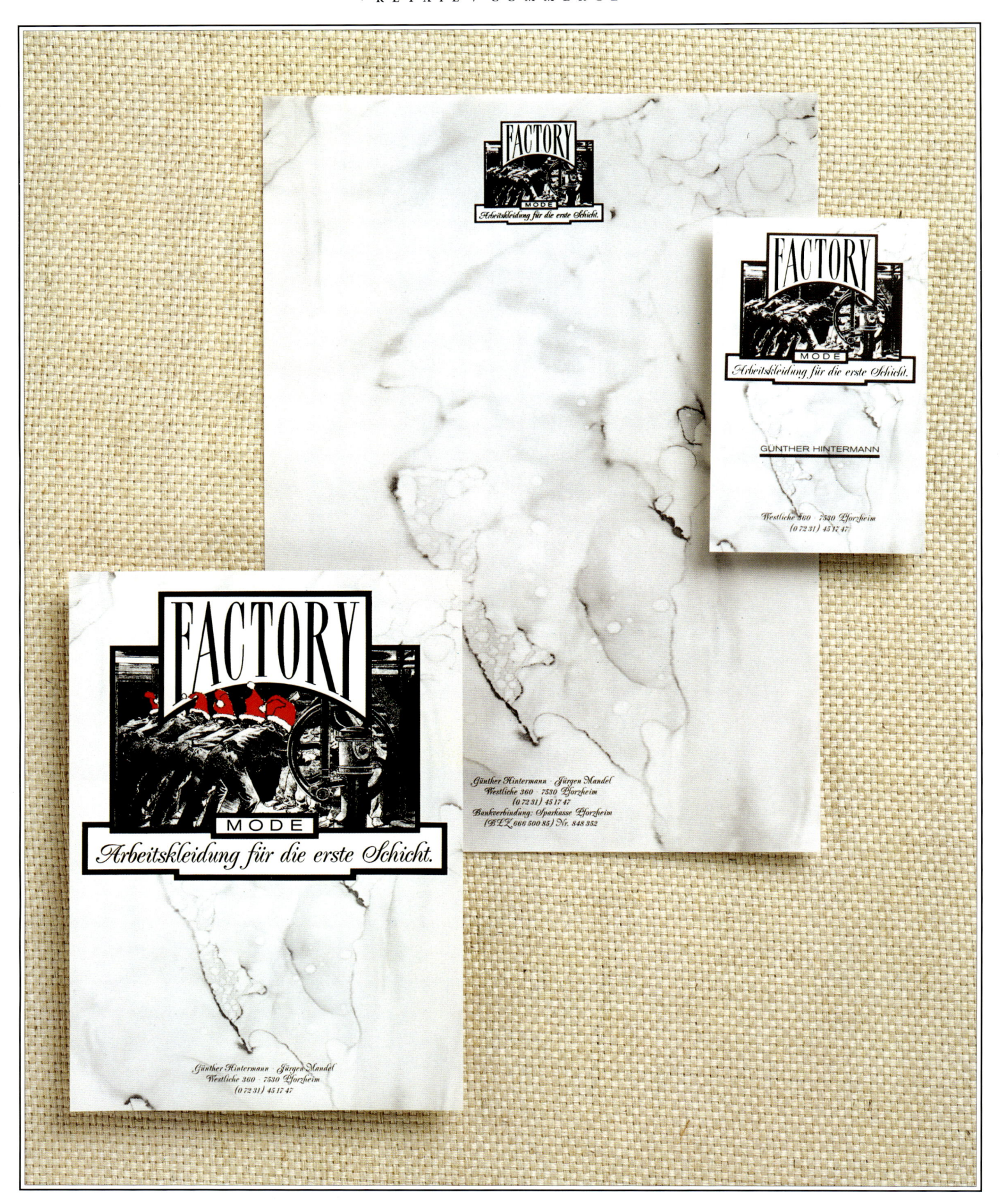

FACTORY Fashion Shop ファッションショップ GERMANY 1989 CD: Thomas Feicht AD, D, I: Peter Hinz CW: Ralf Merboth DF: Trust Corporate Culture

SASCHA FASHION DESIGN Fashion for Men & Women, Italian & French Collection イタリア、フランスの紳士、婦人服 THE NETHERLANDS 1992 D, I: Luc Reefman Bno DF: KBO & R Design

• RETAIL / COMMERCE •

MIKI CO, LTD.   Jewelry Shop   宝石店   JAPAN   1991   AD: Douglas Dollittle

• RETAIL / COMMERCE •

KIMURA KOHKI CO, LTD. Inported Bag Shop 輸入バッグ販売 JAPAN 1992 CD: Nio Kimura AD, D: Masayuki Shimuzu DF: Heter-O-Doxy Protprast

• RETAIL / COMMERCE •

LILO OPERA Fashion Shop ファッションショップ GERMANY 1990 CD: Thomas Feicht AD, D, I: Regina Reiling CW: Ralf Merboth DF: Trust Corporate

• RETAIL / COMMERCE •

GERY ROEKENS / HET BURGER MEESTERS HUYS Belgian Restaurant   ベルギー料理レストラン   THE NETHERLANDS 1993
D: Luc Reefman Bno / Klaas Jan Woudsma Bno   P: Mariolein Van Den Bos   DF: KBO & R Design

• RETAIL / COMMERCE •

STIL + BLÜTE, SILVIA RIEMANN + UTE REUSSENZEHN Flower Shop 花屋 GERMANY 1990 CD: Thomas Feicht AD, D, I: Sudith Heinz DF: Trust Corporate Culture

• RETAIL / COMMERCE •

POWDER Apparel Maker and Shop 婦人服製造、販売 JAPAN 1989-1993 D: Hideki Shimosako

• RETAIL / COMMERCE •

VAZARA Hair & Make up   ヘア ＆ メイク   JAPAN 1991   AD, D: Yoshiro Kajitani   D: Michiko Arakawa   P: Hitoshi Iwakiri   DF: Kajitani Design Room

• RETAIL / COMMERCE •

CHEZ LAHLOU   French, Italian Restaurant   フランス、イタリア料理レストラン   UK 1992   AD, D, I: The Designers Republic   DF: The Designers Republic

ZONK, INC.   Screen Printed Activewear   スクリーンプリントの活動服販売   USA 1990   CD: Greg Sabin   D, I: Tracy Sabin   DF: Sabin Design

• RETAIL / COMMERCE •

HONG KONG SEIBU ENTERPRISE CO., LTD.　Department Store　百貨店　HONG KONG　1991　AD, D: Alan Chan　D: Phillip Leung　I: Gary Cheung　DF: Alan Chan Design

TAKEO CO., LTD.　Paper Wholesaler　洋紙卸売業　JAPAN　1991　CD: Tsuyokatsu Kudo　AD, D: Yuriko Tomita　D: Design Laboratory　DF: Design Laboratory

• RETAIL / COMMERCE •

JOYCE BOUTIQUE LIMITED Fashion Boutique ファッションブティック HONG KONG 1990 AD, D: Alan Chan D: Phillip Leung DF: Alan Chan Design

• RETAIL / COMMERCE •

OPTIK ISELIN Exclusive Retailer of Glasses 高級メガネ販売 SWITZERLAND 1991 AD, D, I: Christian Hügin DF: Christian Hügin

TAKEO CO., LTD. Paper Wholesaler 洋紙卸売業 JAPAN 1991 CD: Tsuyokatsu Kudo AD: Nobuyoshi Kikuchi D: Design Laboratory DF: Design Laboratory

• RETAIL / COMMERCE •

BOWHAUS Rental Photo Studio 貸撮影室 USA 1992 D: Margo Chase / Alan Disparte DF: Margo Chase Design

• 138 •

• RETAIL / COMMERCE •

THE KYOTO HOTEL LTD.   Hotel   ホテル   JAPAN   1993   AD: GK Kyoto / Daisuke Nakatsuka   D: Yasuhiko Matsumoto / Masami Ishibashi   DF: Nakatsuka Daisuke
JOAN GARCIA ARGELAGUET   Wool Buyer   羊毛仕入れ業   UK   1989   AD, D: Teresa Roviras   DF: Teresa Roviras

• RETAIL / COMMERCE •

COLLEGE POSTERS + PRINTS   Poster and Art Print Merchandisers   ポスター、アートプリント商品取扱い   UK 1990   AD, D: The Designers Republic   DF: The Designers Republic

• RETAIL / COMMERCE •

801 STEAK AND CHOP HOUSE　Restaurant　レストラン　USA　1993　AD, D, I: John Sayles　DF: Sayles Graphic Design

• 141 •

• MANUFACTURING / PRODUCTS •

I. A. BEDFORD　Textile Manufacturer　テキスタイル製造　USA　1992　AD, D, I: John Sayles　CW: Wendy Lyons　DF: Sayles Graphic Design

• MANUFACTURING / PRODUCTS •

ROSS SUTHERLAND Farm 農場 USA 1992 CD: James M. Skiles AD: Kathryn Klein D: Tim McGrath

• 143 •

• MANUFACTURING / PRODUCTS •

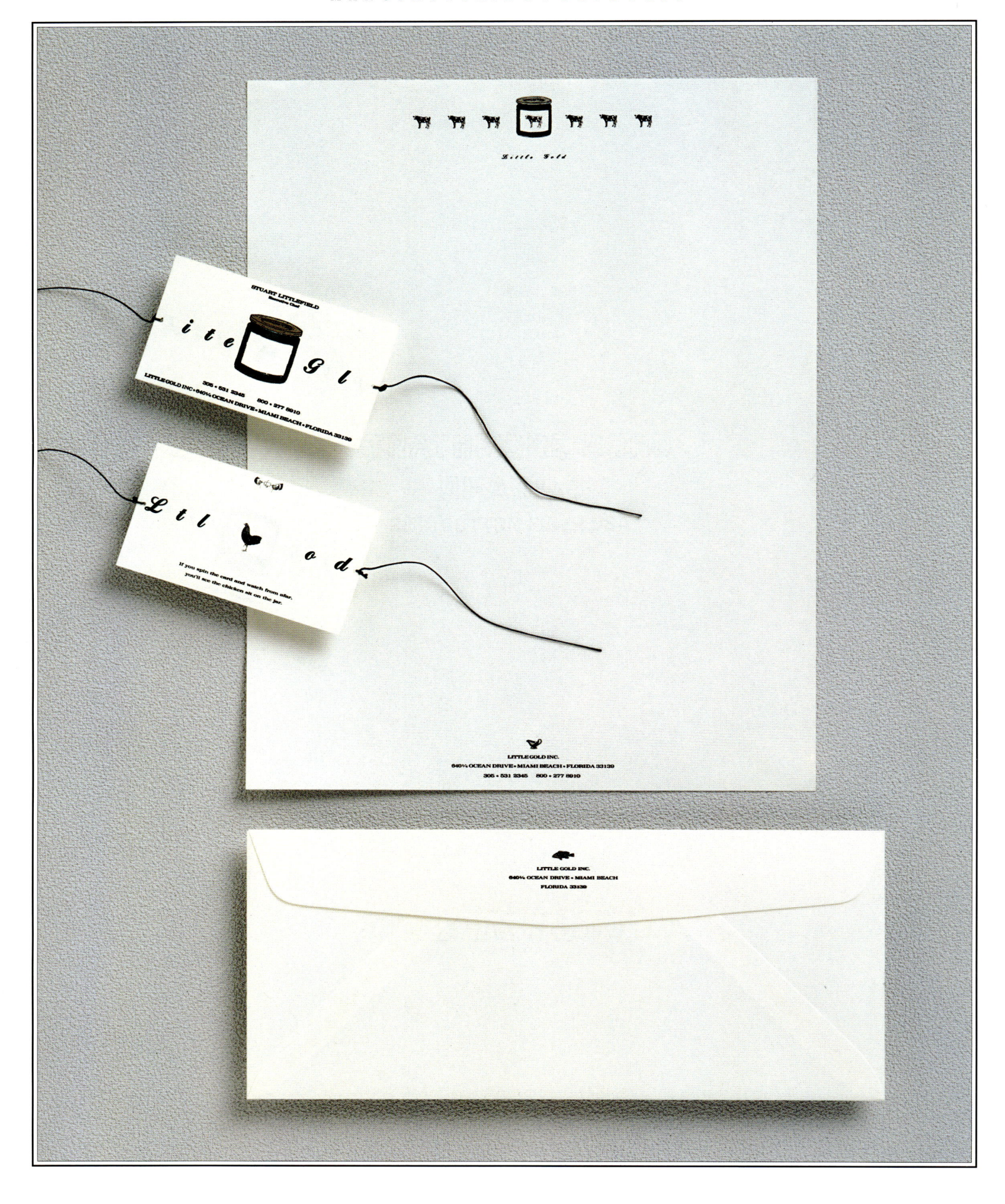

LITTLE GOLD   Soup-base Manufacturer   スープの素製造   HONG KONG   1989   AD, D, I: Stefan Sagmeister   DF: Sagmeister Graphics

• MANUFACTURING / PRODUCTS •

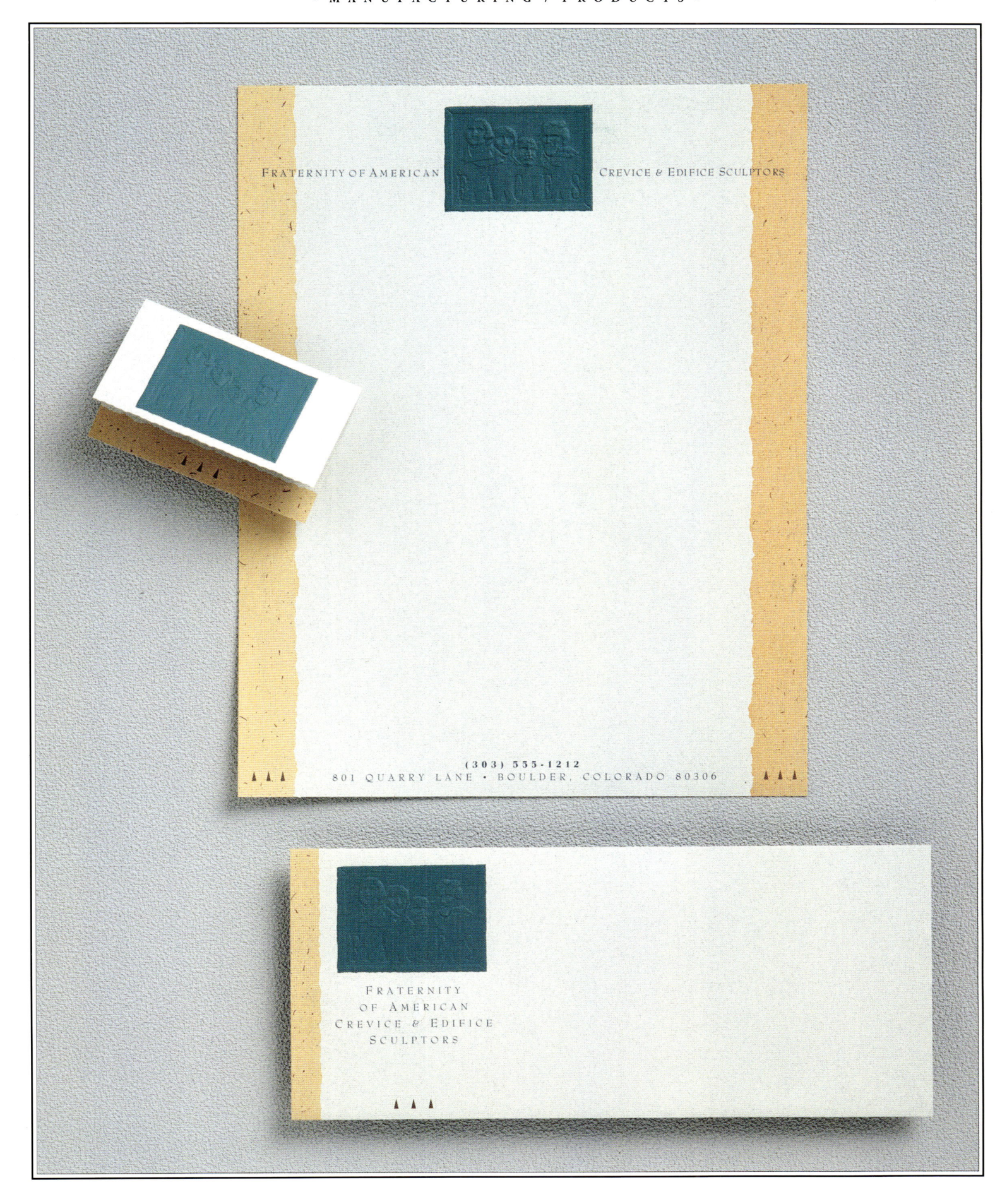

THE BECKETY PAPER COMPANY Paper Manufacturer 紙製造 USA 1989 AD, D: Eric Rickabaugh DF: Rickabaugh Graphics
Special Effects: Trademark has been embossed. マークが型押しされている。

• MANUFACTURING / PRODUCTS •

PRINT CRAFT, INC. Printer 印刷業 USA 1989 AD, D: Charles Spencer Anderson D: Daniel Olson DF: Charles S. Anderson Design
BROOKS HOWARD Duplicator 複製業 USA 1991 AD, D: Stan Evenson D: Glenn Sakamoto

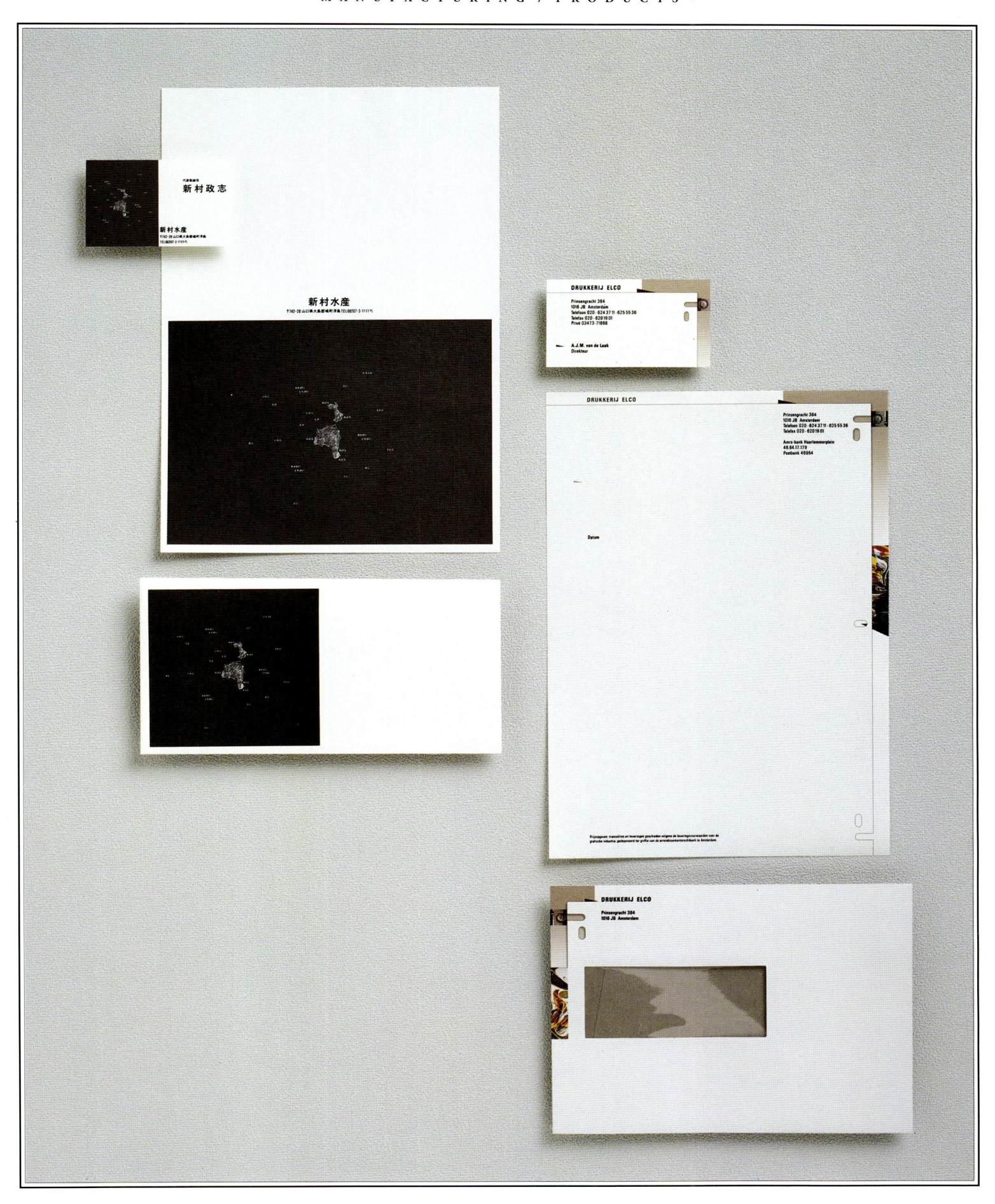

SHINMURA SUISAN Marine Products Industry 水産業 JAPAN 1991 AD, D: Norito Shinmura CW: Kazutaka Sato
DRUKKERIJ ELCO Printer 印刷業 THE NETHERLANDS 1991 AD, D: Anton Vos DF: Dedato

JAQUET PARQUET AG Exclusive Parquet Firm 高級寄せ木細工 SWITZERLAND 1990 AD, D: Christian Hügin P: Felix Strfuli CW: Roland Mùllek Muller DF: Christian Hügin

• MANUFACTURING / PRODUCTS •

CURRAN ART GLASS Maker of Fine Glass ファインガラス製造 USA 1991 CD: Mark Oldach AD, D: Don Emery P: Bob Huff DF: Mark Oldach Design

• 149 •

• PROFESSIONAL •

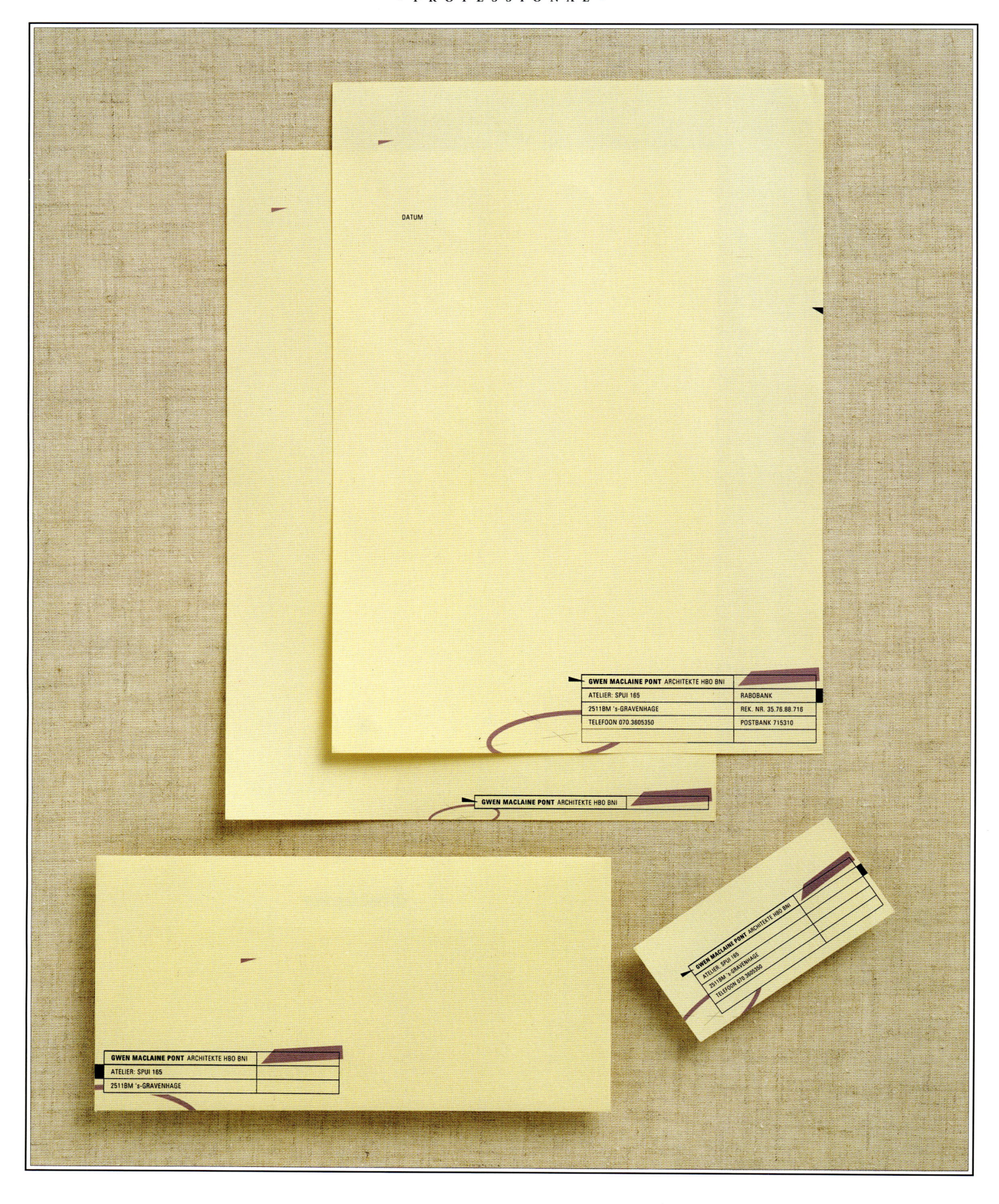

GWEN MACLAINE PONT   Architect   建築家   THE NETHERLANDS   1990   AD, D: Anton Vos   DF: Anton Vos

• PROFESSIONAL •

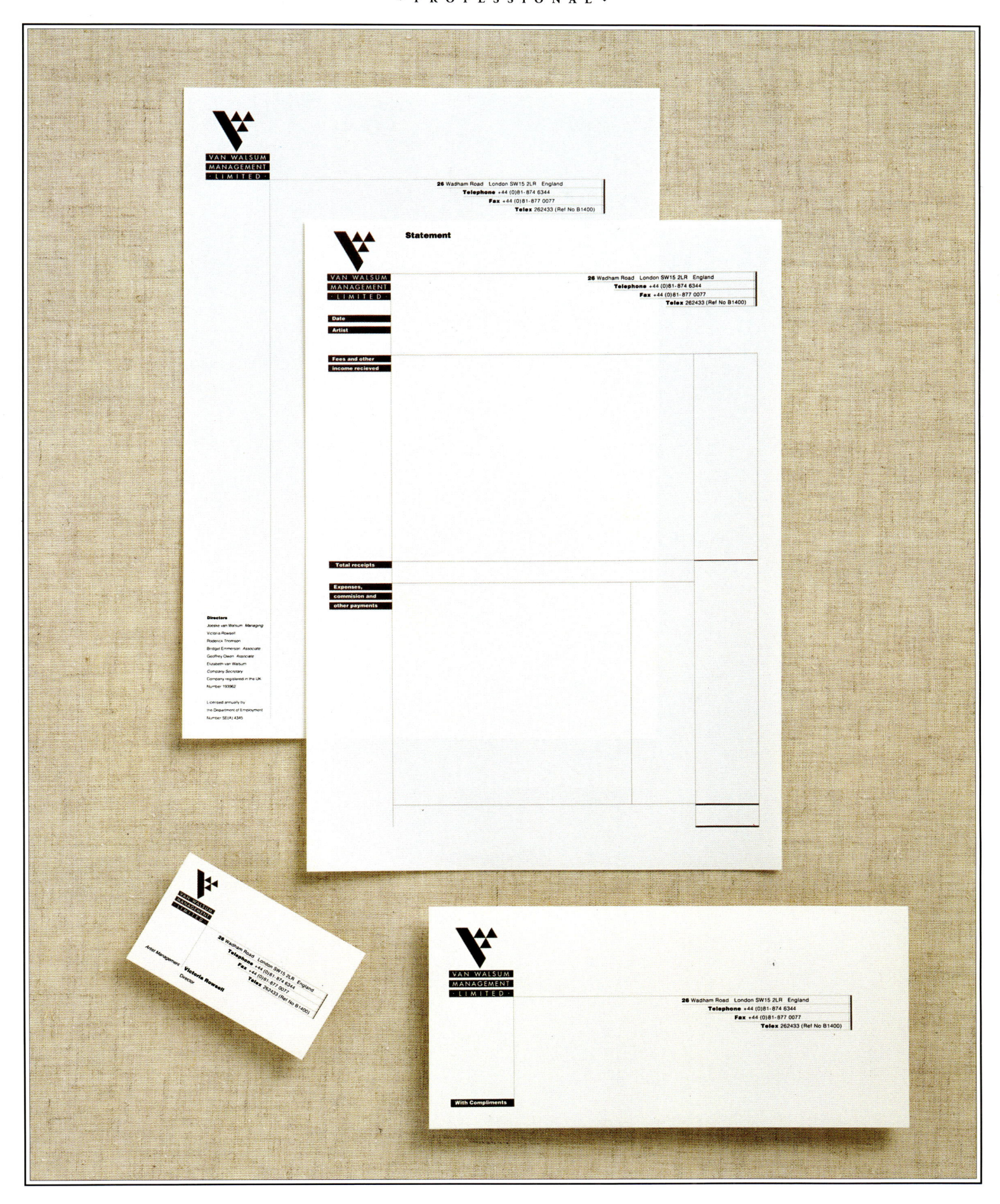

VAN WALSUM MANAGEMENT   Musical Artist Agents, Management and Promotion   ミュージシャンの管理、促進   UK 1992   D: Richard Ward   DF: The Team

• P R O F E S S I O N A L •

MAHLUM & NORDFORS MCKINLEY GORDON Architecture 建築設計 USA 1993 AD, D: Jack Anderson D: Scott Eggers / Leo Raymundo DF: Hornall Anderson Design Works

• PROFESSIONAL •

IOWA HEALTH RESEARCH INSTITUTE   Medical Scientific Research Organization   医療科学研究協会   USA 1992   AD, D, I: John Sayles   DF: Sayles Graphic Design

• PROFESSIONAL •

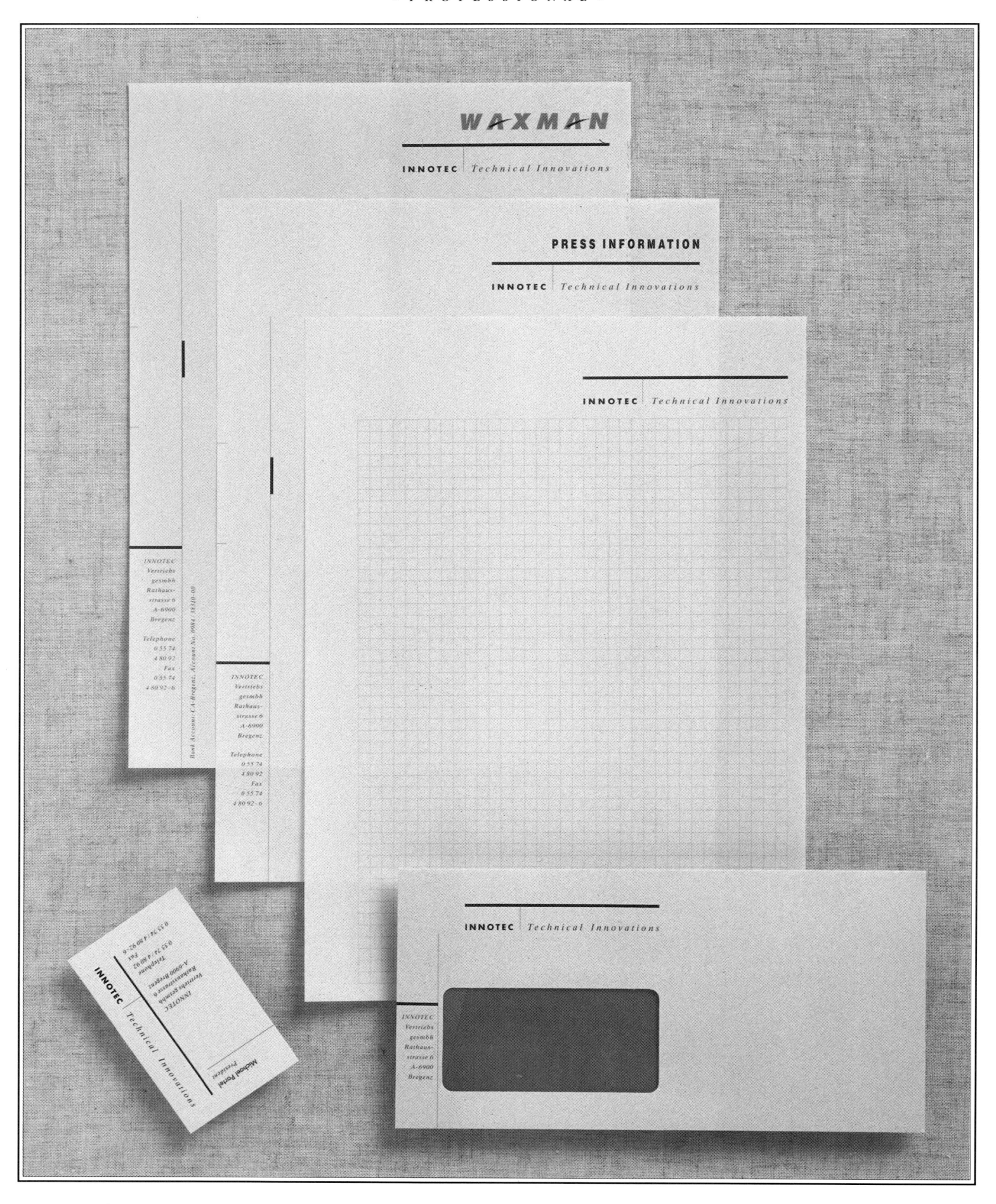

INNOTEC GMBH　Technical Innovations　技術革新業　AUSTRIA　1992　D: Kurt Dornig　DF: Dornig Grafik Design

• PROFESSIONAL •

BARTHOLOMÄUS MOOSBRUGGER   Architect   建築家   AUSTRIA   1992   AD, D, I: Sigi Ramoser   DF: Sigi Ramoser

• P R O F E S S I O N A L •

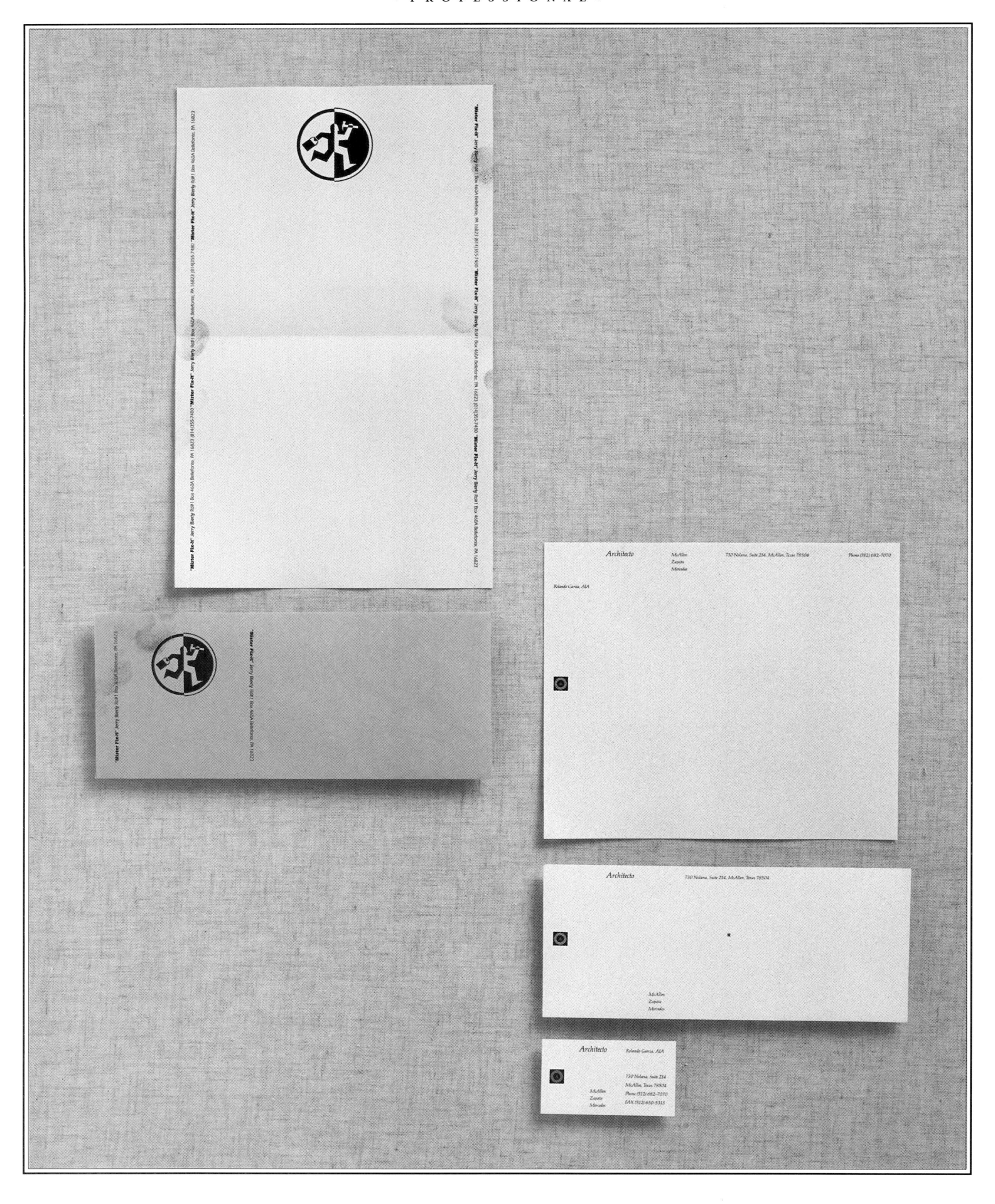

MISTER FIX - IT   General Repairs Contractor   一般修理、土建業   USA 1991   AD, D: Kristin Sommese   AD, I: Canny Sommese   DF: Sommese Design

ARCHITECTO   Architectural Engineering   建築設計工学   USA 1989   AD, D, I, CW: Charles Hively

• P R O F E S S I O N A L •

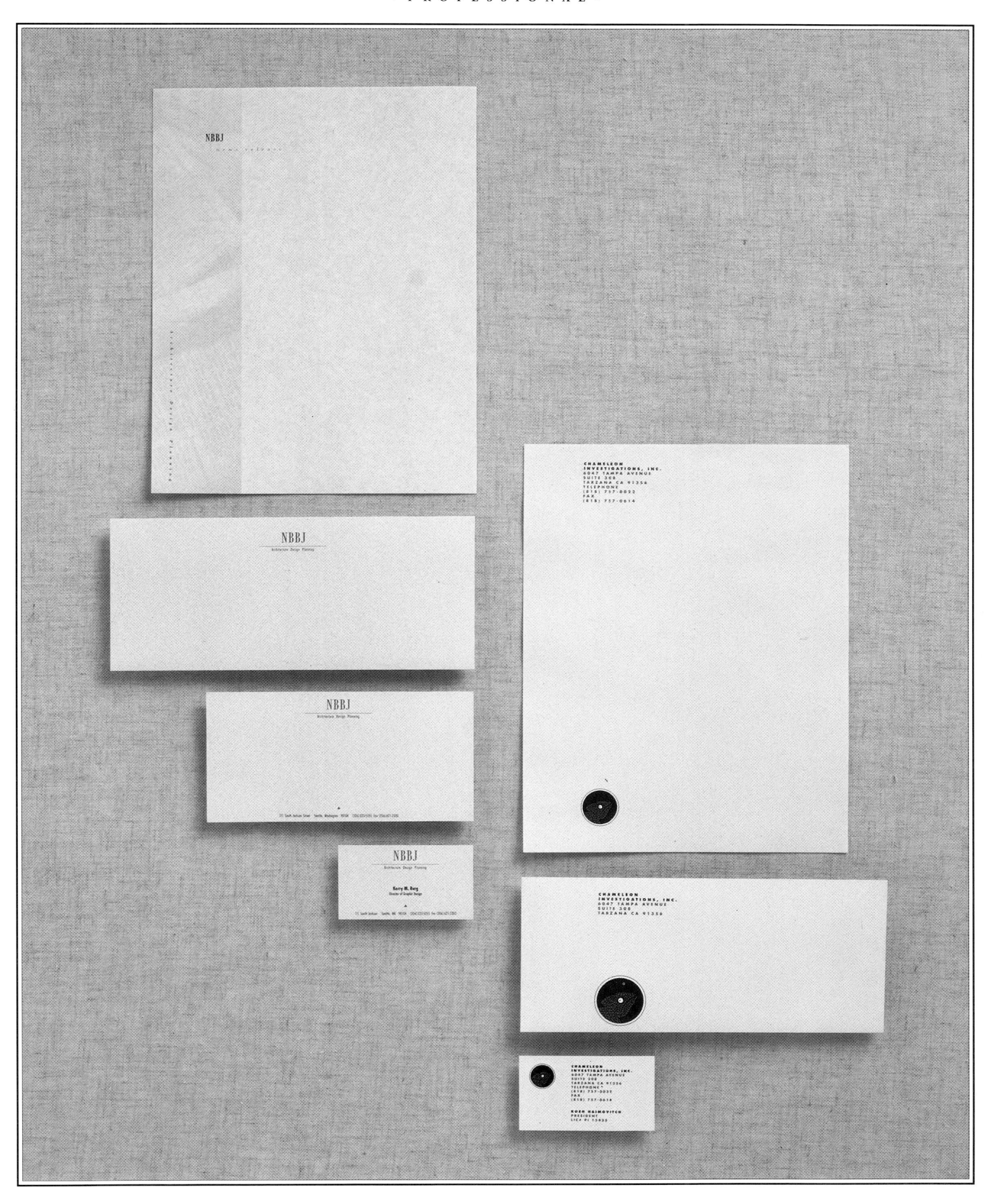

NBBJ Architecture, Design and Planning 建築設計、デザイン、プランニング USA 1990 CD: Kerry Burg D: Doug Keyes / Stefanie Choi / Margo Sepanski / Susan Dewey DF: NBBJ - Graphic Design
CHAMELEON INVESTIGATIONS, INC. Private Investigations and Corporate Security 個人調査、企業保護サービス USA 1992 AD, D, I: Peter Bradford DF: Peter Bradford and Associates

• PROFESSIONAL •

DOUGLAS K. LARSON, D. D. S Dentist 歯科医 USA 1986 D: Lauren Smith DF: Lauren Smith Design
BECKLEY IMPORTS, INC. Car Repair Service 車修理サービス USA 1993 AD, D, I: John Sayles DF: Sayles Graphic Design

• PROFESSIONAL •

HOOGSTRATEN PARTNERS Consultancy Organization コンサルタント協会 THE NETHERLANDS 1991 D: Luc Reefman Bno DF: KBO & R Design

• PROFESSIONAL •

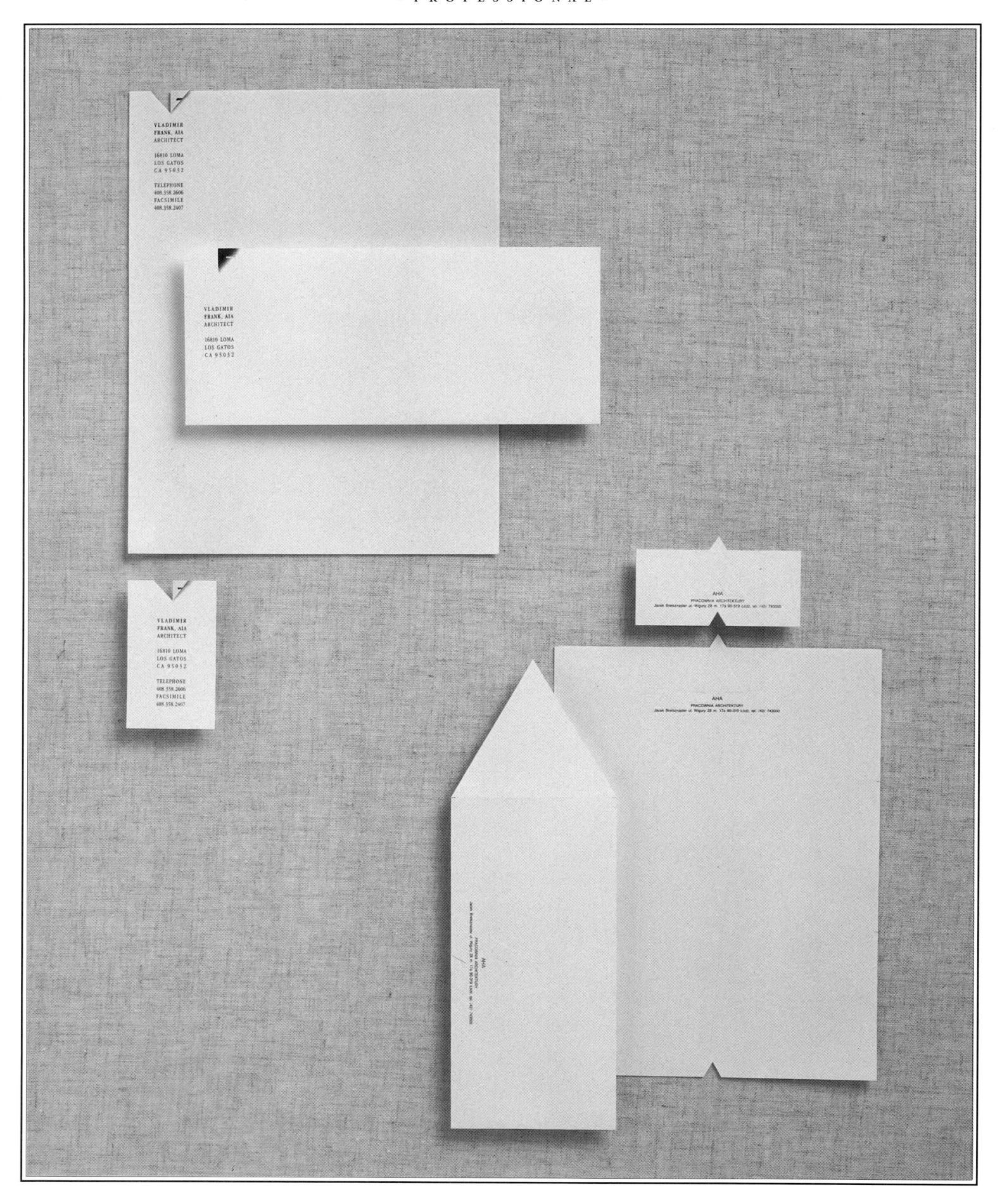

V. FRANK, AIA Architect 建築家 USA 1993 AD, D: Iva Frank DF: Iva Frank Graphic Design
AHA-JACEK BRETSZNAJDER Architecture 建築設計 POLAND 1990 AD, D: Tadeusz Piechura DF: Atelier Tadeusz Piechura

• PROFESSIONAL •

PARADIGM HEALTH CORP.   Health Care   ヘルスケア   USA   1991   AD, D: Neal Zimmermann   DF: Zimmermann Crowe Design
JOHN F. KILEY Ⅲ CPA   Certified Public Accountants   公認会計士   USA   1991   AD, D: Teddie Barnhart   DF: Barnstorming Designs

• P R O F E S S I O N A L •

ROMY SIEBER (MRS.) ZÜRICH Career Management for Women 女性の職業管理 SWITZERLAND 1991 AD, I, CW: Michael Baviera D: Siegrun Nuber DF: BBV

• PROFESSIONAL •

BECKER - KORREKTUREN   Proofreader   校正者   GERMANY 1989   CD: Thomas Feicht   AD, D: Willie Demel   P: Bernd Mayer   DF: Trust Corporate Culture

DALE F. STEELE   Fashion Consultant   ファッション・コンサルタント   USA 1990   AD, D: Iva Frank   DF: Iva Frank Graphic Design

• P R O F E S S I O N A L •

KOKI KOGEI INC. Display Business ディスプレイ、施工 JAPAN 1991 AD, D: Eiichi Sakota D: Toshio Kawakami DF: Rec 2nd

• P R O F E S S I O N A L •

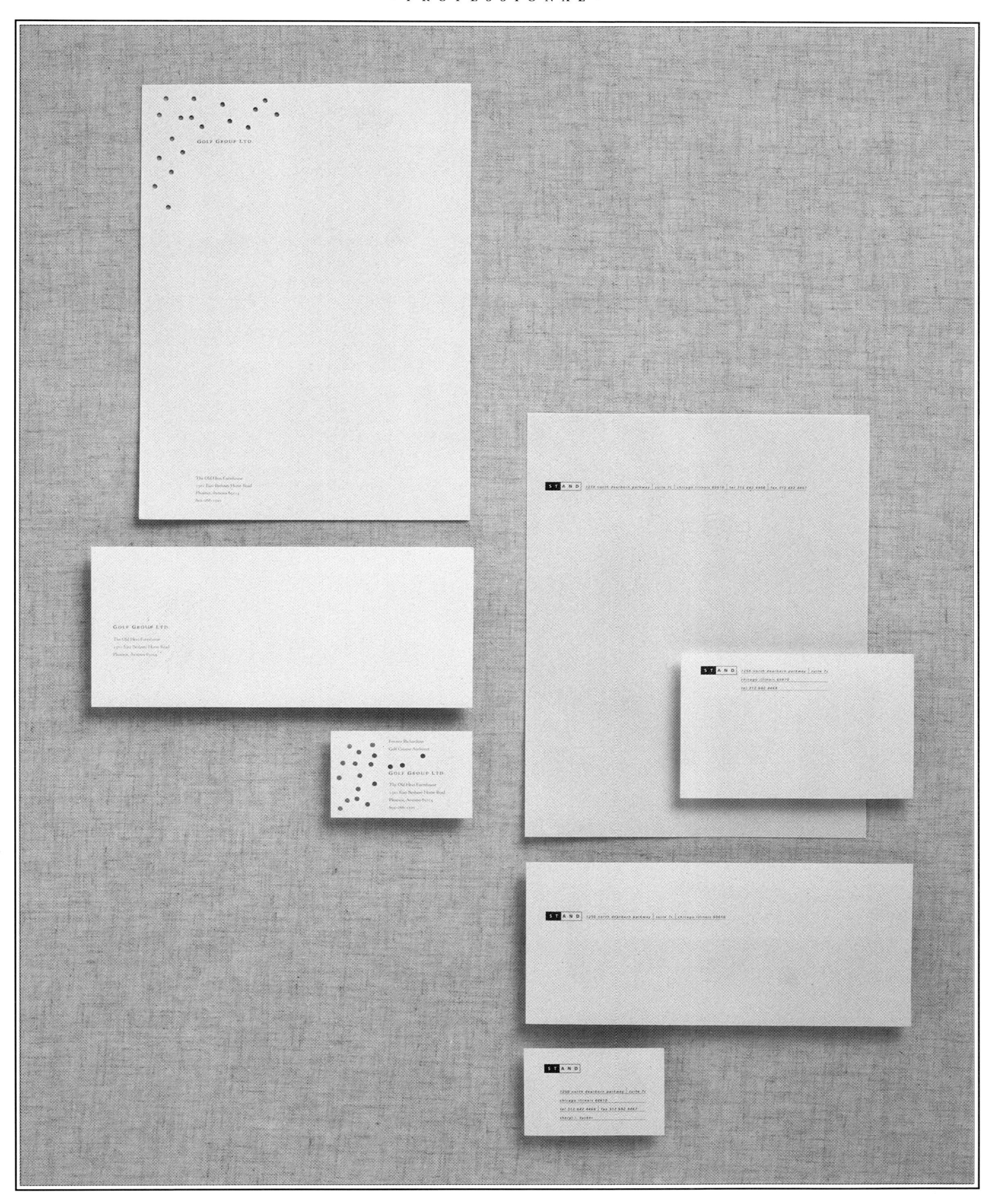

GOLF GROUP LTD. Golf Course Architects ゴルフコース設計 USA 1988 AD, D: Forrest Richardson DF: Richardson or Richardson

STAND Entrepreneur with Several Businesses 数種職業の仲介 USA 1992 D: Jilly Simons DF: Concrete, Chicago

• PROFESSIONAL •

ARMIN SCHNEIDER   Badminton Trainer   バドミントンコーチ   HONG KONG 1990   CD, D, I: Stefan Sagmeister   DF: Sagmeister Graphics

• P R O F E S S I O N A L •

PAUL BARGEHR   Massage Parlour   マッサージ営業所   AUSTRIA   1992   AD, D: Sigi Ramoser   DF: Sigi Ramoser

• PROFESSIONAL •

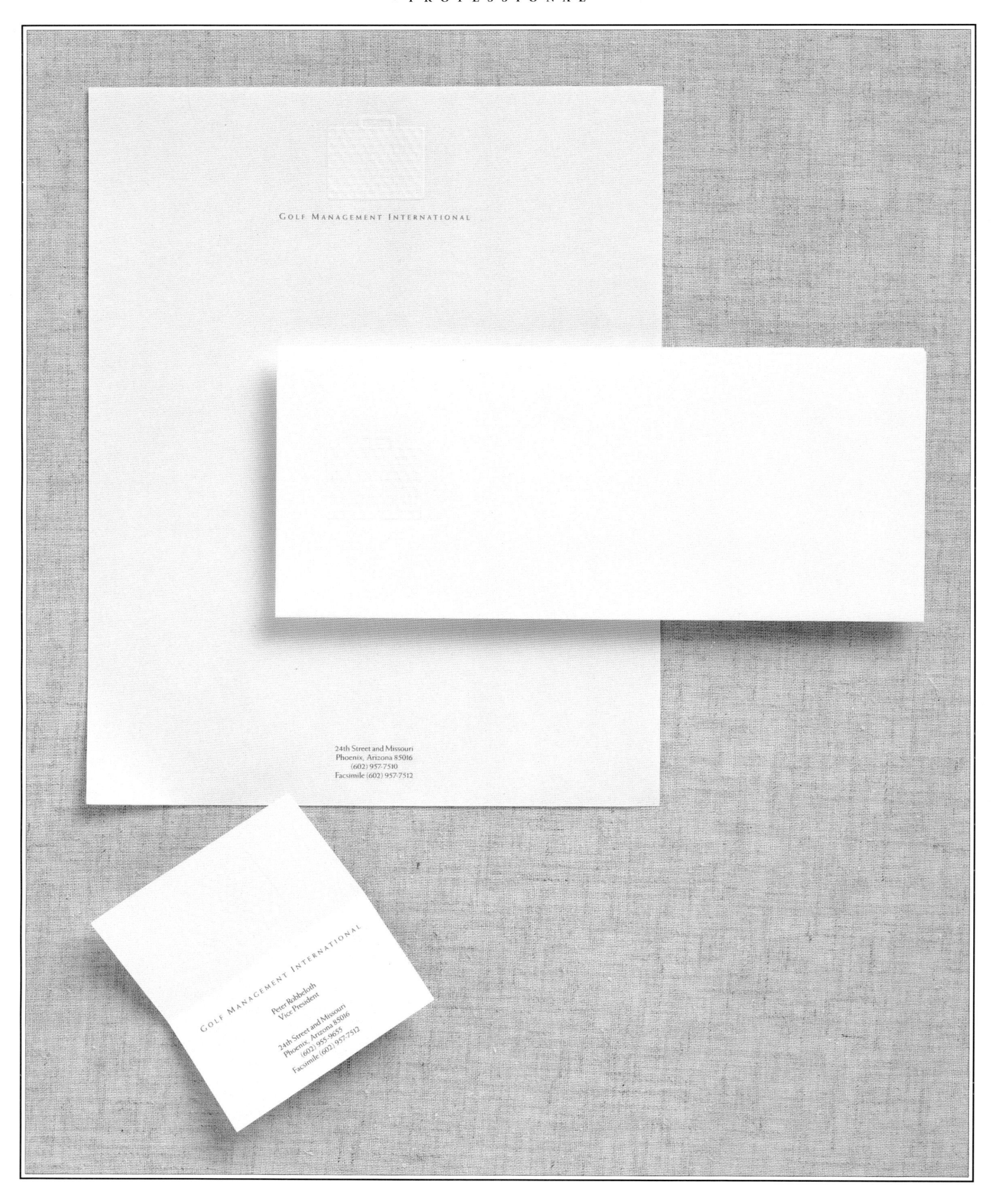

GOLF MANAGEMENT INTERNATIONAL Golf Development and Management ゴルフの管理、推進 USA 1990
CD: Forrest Richardson AD, D: Debi Young Mees I: Jim Bolek DF: Richardson or Richardson

• PROFESSIONAL •

DAVID WARREN DESIGN Graphic Design グラフィックデザイン USA AD, D: David Warren P: Jim Havey DF: David Warren Design

• PROFESSIONAL •

IDEAPAJA   Model Making   モデルメイキング   FINLAND   1988   D, I: Viktor Kaltala   DF: Viktorno Design

DR. GÜNTER LUDESCHER Dentist 歯科医 AUSTRIA 1991 D: Kurt Dornig DF: Dornig Grafik Design

• PROFESSIONAL •

COLOR CONTROL Color Separation and Prepress   印刷前の色分解   USA 1992 AD, D: Rick Eiber   DF: Rick Eiber Design (Red)

YOUNG PRESIDENT'S ORGANIZATION Association of Corporate Presidents 企業主協会 USA
AD: John Waters   D: Margaret Riegal   CW: Young President's Organization   DF: Waters Design Associates

KAB, INC. (RYUICHI SAKAMOTO)　Promotion and Management　アーティストの管理、促進　USA　1993　CD: Robert Bergman-Ungar　D: Liong The

• PROFESSIONAL •

UP & RUNNING, INC.　Computer Based Fitness Service　コンピュータ処理のフィットネスサービス　USA　1989　CD: Kim Youngblood　P: Eadweard Muybridge　DF: Youngblood, Sweat & Tears

TOHTORE CO., LTD.　Produce　プロデュース　JAPAN　1990　AD, D: Keisuke Unosawa　DF: Keisuke Unosawa Design

• PROFESSIONAL •

EAGLE LAKE ON ORCAS ISLAND　Island Development　島開発　USA　1992　AD, D, I: Julia LaPine　D, LETTERER: Denise Weir　DF: Hornall Anderson Design Works

• PROFESSIONAL •

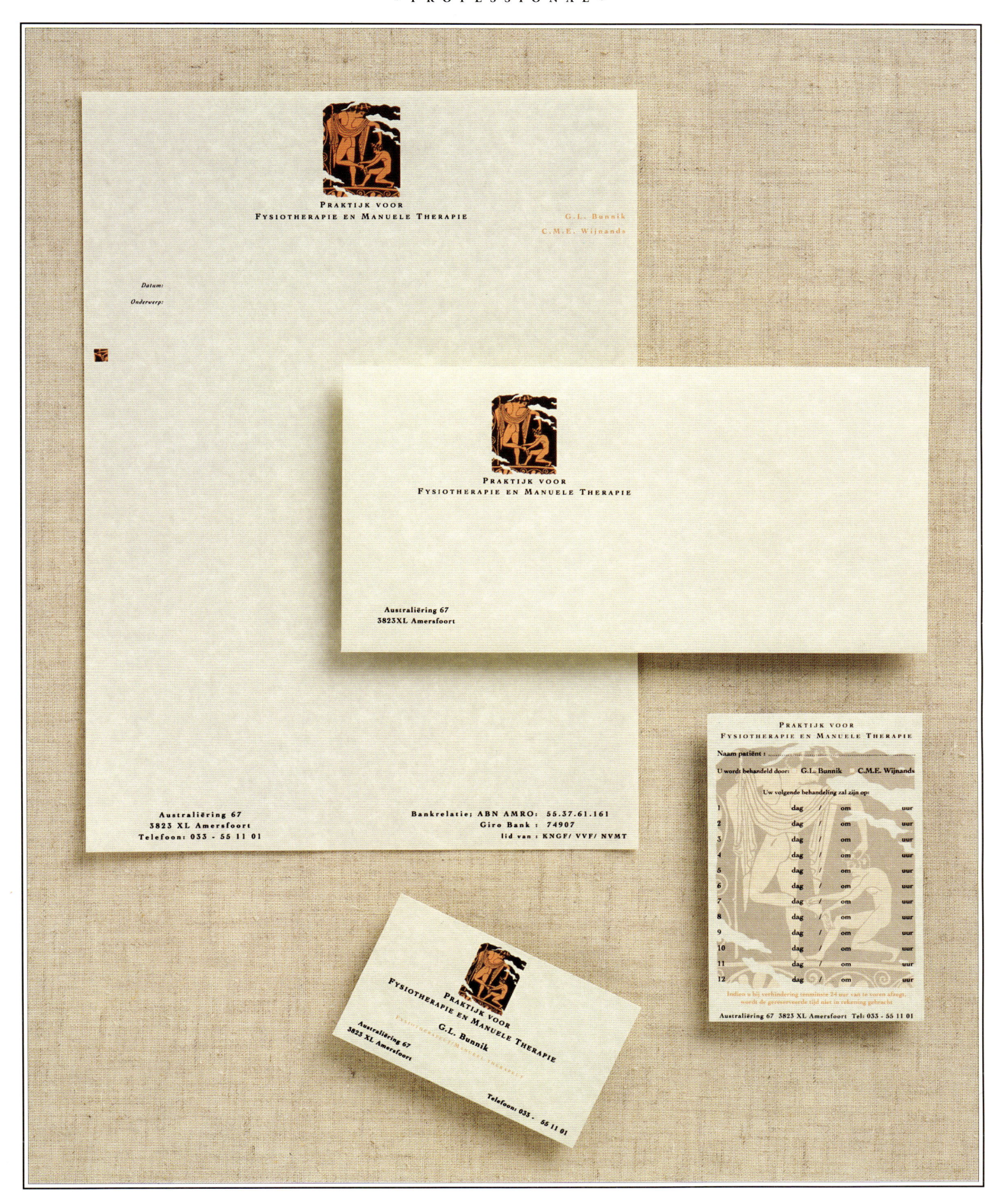

ERWIN WIJNANDS & LEX BUNNIK Physiotherapy and Manual Therapy 物理療法、手動療法 THE NETHERLANDS 1992 D, I: Luc Reefman Bno DF: KBO & R Design

• PROFESSIONAL •

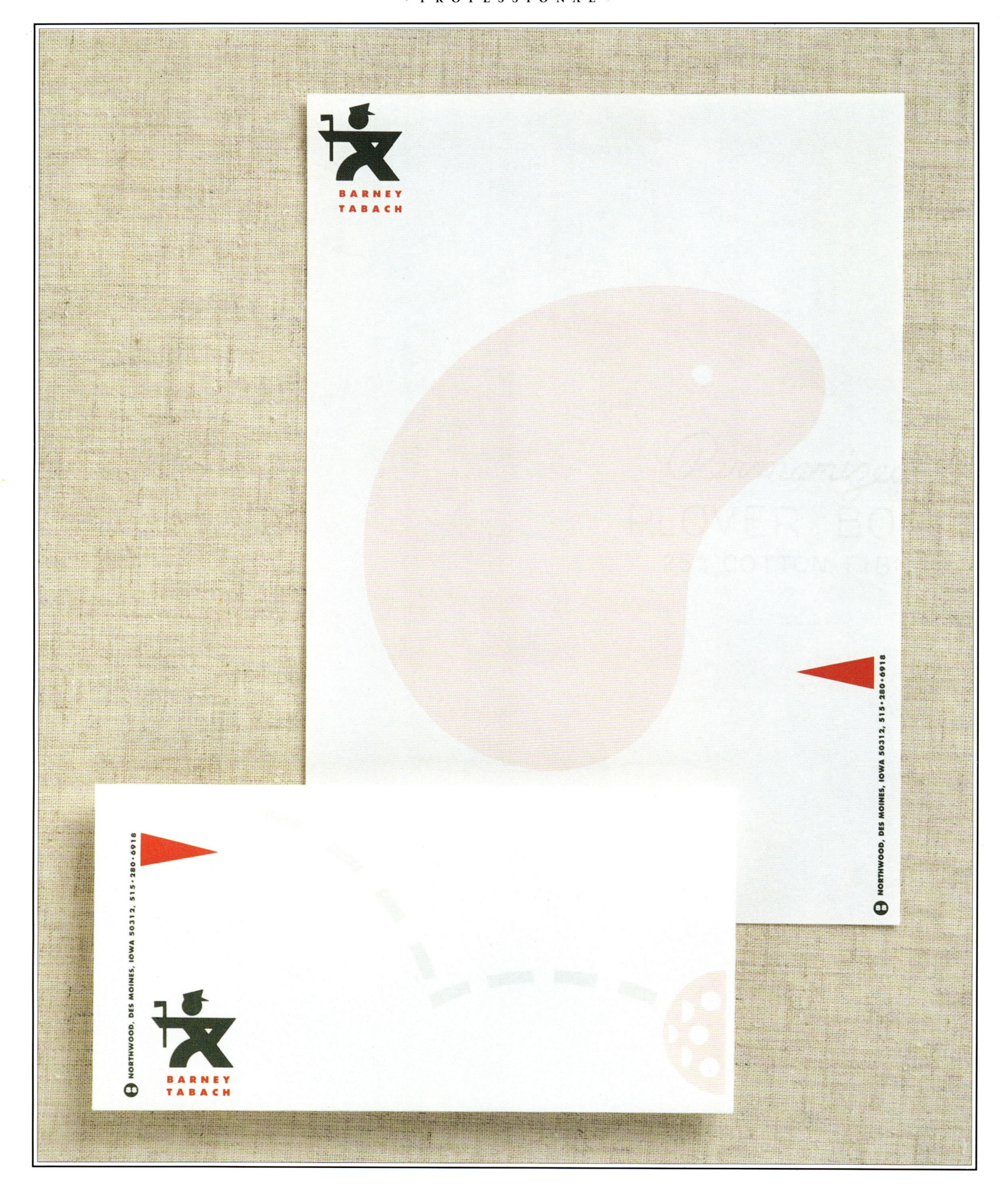

BARNEY TABACH, AVID Golfer (personal) ゴルファー USA 1992 AD, D, I: John Sayles DF: Sayles Graphic Design

• PROFESSIONAL •

SPORTS TURF DYNAMICS　Designers and Installers of Turf Management Systems　芝生管理装置のデザイン、設計　AUSTRALIA　1991　D, I: David Roffey　DF: David Roffey Design

• PROFESSIONAL •

b³ BLUMENTHAL   Office Communication   オフィス通信サービス   GERMANY 1992   AD, D: Detlef Behr   DF: Detlef Behr, Graphik-design

• PROFESSIONAL •

CURATOR OFFICE INC. Curator キュレーター JAPAN 1992 AD, D: Tatsuaki Yasuno DF: T. Y. D.

◆ PROFESSIONAL ◆

QUADRANT RESEARCH & DEVELOPMENT LTD　Systems Software Research and Development　システムソフトウェアの研究開発　UK 1993
AD, D: The Designers Republic　DF: The Designers Republic

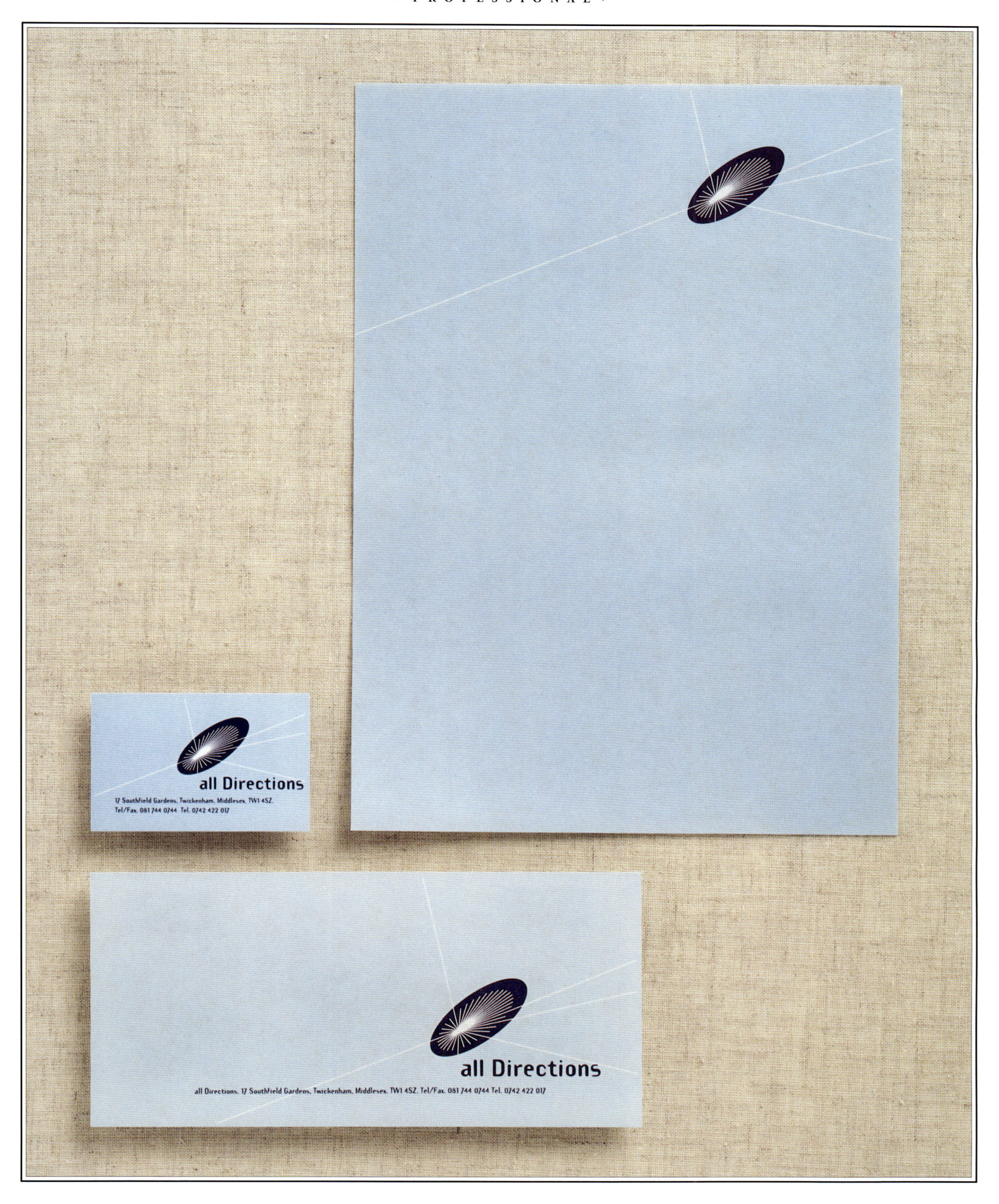

• P R O F E S S I O N A L •

ALL DIRECTIONS   Theatrical Agents and Artist Management   劇団取次、アーティスト管理   UK 1992   AD, D: The Designers Republic   DF: The Designers Republic

• PROFESSIONAL •

KURTZ MANN   Mural Painters and Wall Decorators   壁のペイント、壁面装飾   CANADA 1991   AD, D: Del Terrelonge   I: Kurtz Mann studio   DF: Terrelonge Design
Special Effects: Black and varniched lettering have been overlaid on a patterned background.   地模様の入った紙に黒文字とニス状の文字を重ねている。

• PROFESSIONAL •

DA VINCI GROEP Consultancy in Information Technology   情報技術コンサルタント   THE NETHERLANDS 1991
CD: André Toet   AD, D: Hans Meiboom   I: Leonardo da Vinch   DF: Samenwerkende Ontwerpers

• PROFESSIONAL •

EUROPEAN MARKETING DISTRIBUTION   Finance Organisation   金融協会   AUSTRIA 1991   D: Kurt Dornig   DF: Dornig Grafik Design

• PROFESSIONAL •

CORPORATE WORLD RELOCATION　Relocation Services　引越専門会社　USA　1993　AD, D, I: Stefanie Choi　DF: Stefanie Choi

• P R O F E S S I O N A L •

KATRIN FUCHS Logopaedics 言語医学 AUSTRIA 1992 AD, D, I: Hubert Egartner DF: Egartner Grafik Design Gda
CENTER FOR ORAL AND MAXILLOFACIAL SURGERY Dentristry-Oral and Maxillofacial Surgery 口腔外科医 USA 1991
AD, D: Jack Anderson D: Brian O'Neill / Lian Ng I: John Fretz DF: Hornall Anderson Design Works

• P R O F E S S I O N A L •

INTEGRUS ARCHITECTURE   Architecture   建築設計   USA 1991   AD, D: John Hornall   D: Paula Cox / Brian O'Neill / Lian Ng   DF: Hornall Anderson Design Works
BERGMANN WASMER & ASSOCIATES   Builders and Developers of Environmental Homes   住宅環境の建設、開発   USA 1991   AD, D: David Warren   I: Diego Ruiz   DF: David Warren Design

• SOCIAL / CULTURAL •

ART CENTER ANNUAL FUND, ART CENTER COLLEGE OF DESIGN　Art College　美術専門学校　USA　1991
AD, D: Rebeca Méndez　D: Kevin Downey　P: Steven A. Heller　PRINTER: Typecraft., Pasadena, California

• SOCIAL / CULTURAL •

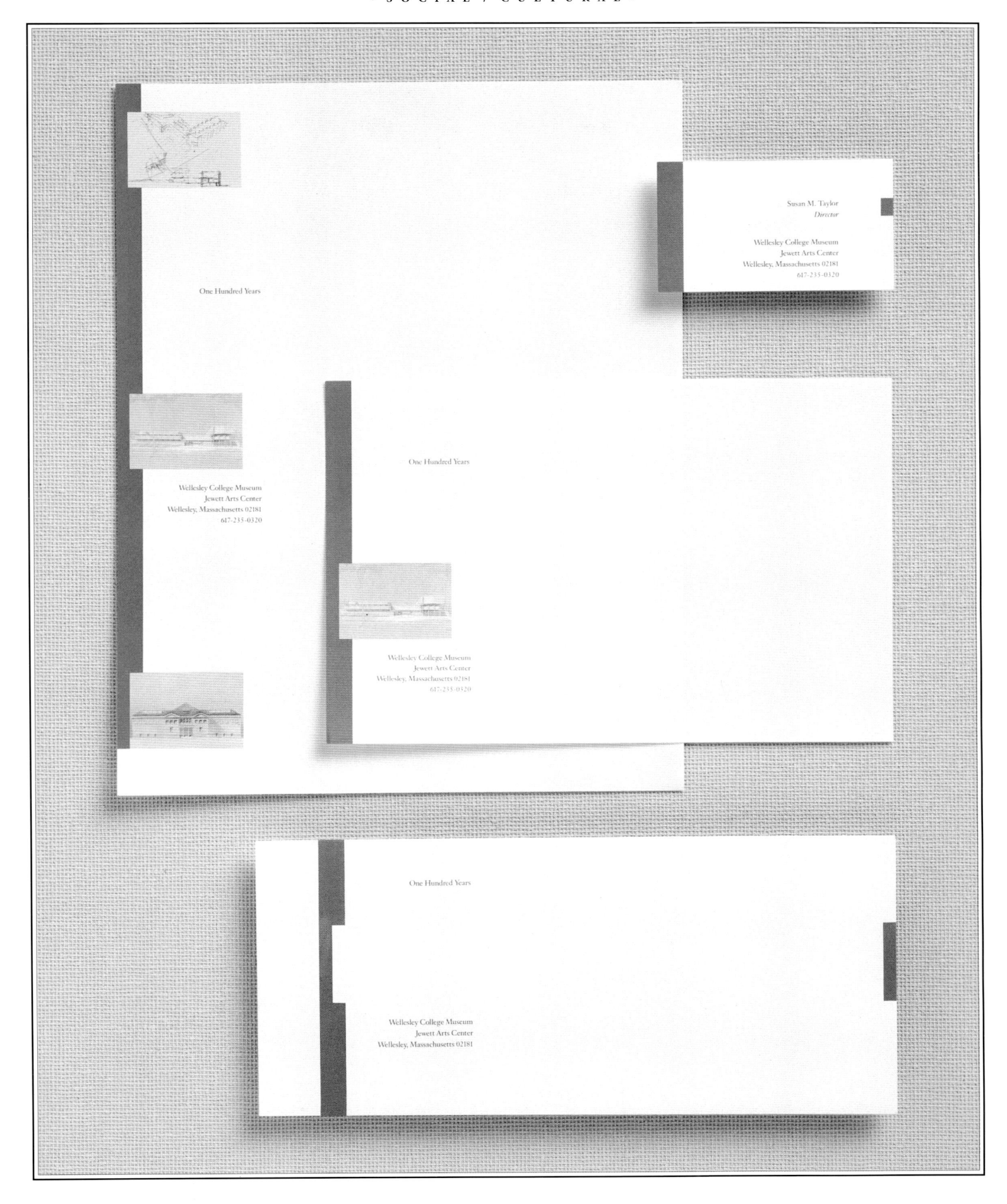

WELLESLEY COLLEGE MUSEUM　Museum　ミュージアム　USA　1989　AD, D: Anita Meyer　I: Jose Rafael Moneo / Paul Rudolph / Rotch and Tilden　DF: plus design

• SOCIAL / CULTURAL •

SQUARE ONE PRESCHOOL Preschool 幼稚園 USA 1985 AD, D: Forrest / Valerie Richardson I: Various Children at the Preschools DF: Richardson or Richardson

• SOCIAL / CULTURAL •

ONE REEL / SEATTLE ARTS COMMISSION   Events Promoter   イベント促進   USA 1993   CD: Kerry Burg   AD, D: Susan Dewey   DF: NBBJ-Graphic Design

• SOCIAL / CULTURAL •

J. W. TUMBLES Children's Gymnastics School 子供の体操学校 USA 1987 AD, D, I: Forrest Richardson AD, D: Valerie Richardson D: Rosemary Connelly DF: Richardson or Richardson

• SOCIAL / CULTURAL •

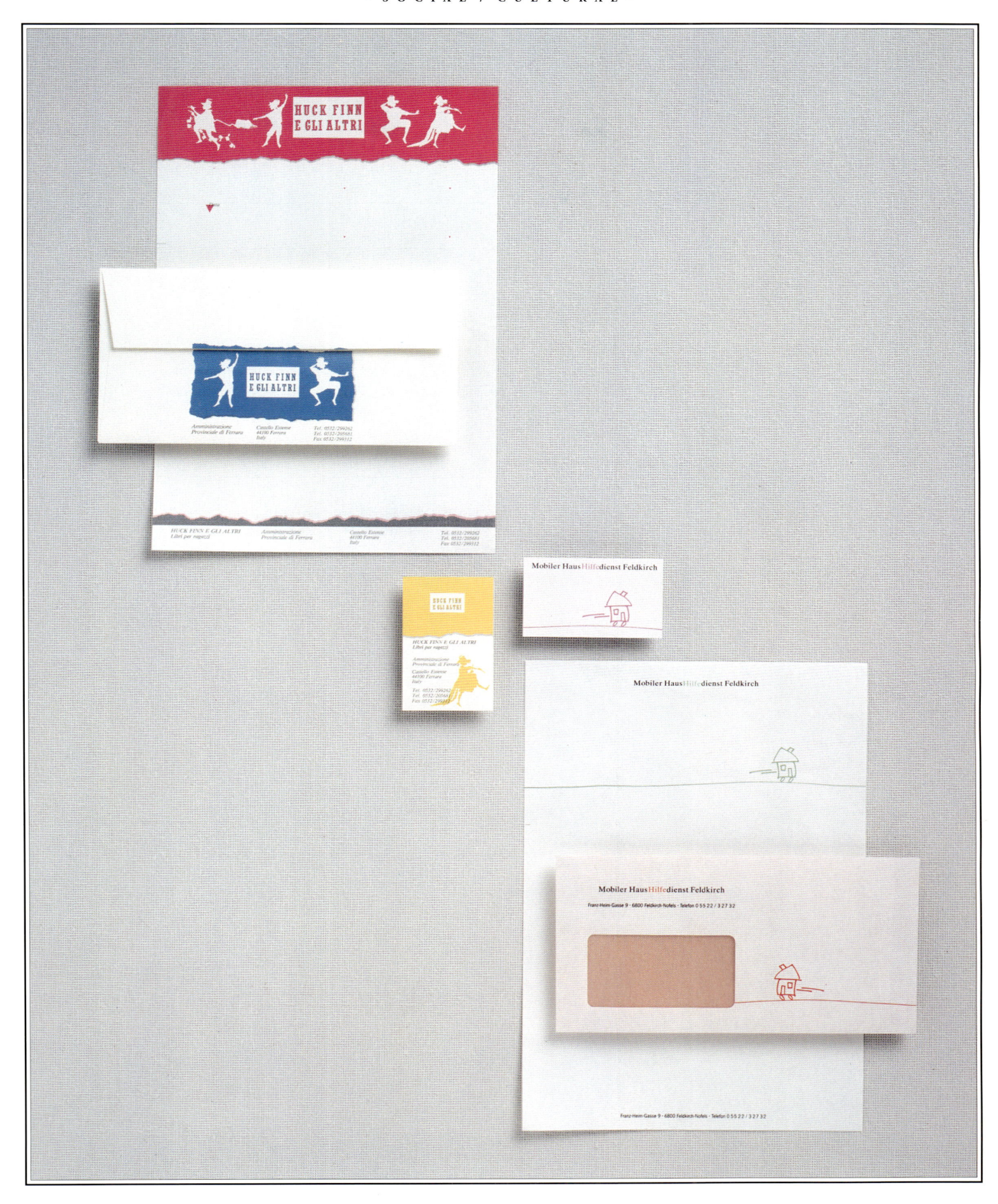

AMM.NE PROVINCIALE DI FERRARA Administration management provinces 地方行政管理 ITALY AD, D, I, CW: Nedda Bonini
MOBILER HAUSHILFEDIENST FELDKIRCH Social Programme Union (helping old and sick people stay home) 社会福祉計画組合（老人や病人の為の滞在所の助力） AUSTRIA 1991
AD, D, I, CW: Sigi Ramoser DF: Aterier Gassner / Schlins-Austria

• SOCIAL / CULTURAL •

UNIVERSITY OF CALIFORNIA, BERKELEY   University   大学   USA   1991   AD, D, I: John Sayles   DF: Sayles Graphic Design

• SOCIAL / CULTURAL •

WESTERN REGIONAL GREEK CONFERENCE   Association of Fraternities and Sororities   男子、女子学生クラブの協会   USA 1991   AD, D, I: John Sayles   DF: Sayles Graphic Design

• SOCIAL / CULTURAL •

UNIVERSITEIT UTRECHT University 大学 THE NETHERLANDS 1992 AD, D: Aad van Dommelen CW: Elsvan Klinken DF: Proforma Rotterdam bNO Association for Design & Consultancy

◆ SOCIAL / CULTURAL ◆

THE CENTER FOR FAMILIES AND CHILDREN　Non-profit Social Service Organization　非営利社会奉仕協会　USA　1993　AD, D: Gail Rigelhaupt　DF: Rigelhaupt Design, NYC

• S O C I A L   /   C U L T U R A L •

WEIDEMAFONDS Foundation 財団 THE NETHERLANDS 1992 CD: André Toet AD, D: Simon Davies CW: Alwin van Steijn DF: Samenwerkende Ontwerpers
ARTS COUNCIL OF GREAT BRITAIN Arts Funding Body アート基金団体 UK 1989 AD, D: The Designers Republic D: Patrick Glower DF: The Designers Republic

• SOCIAL / CULTURAL •

LE BATEAU FEU   Cultural Center   カルチャーセンター   FRANCE 1991   AD, D: Jean-Jacques Tachdjian   DF: I Comme Image

OHIO ARTS COUNCIL   State Council on The Arts   芸術協議会   USA   AD, D: John Waters   D, I: Bob Kellerman   CW: Peter Maloney   DF: Waters Design Associates

• SOCIAL / CULTURAL •

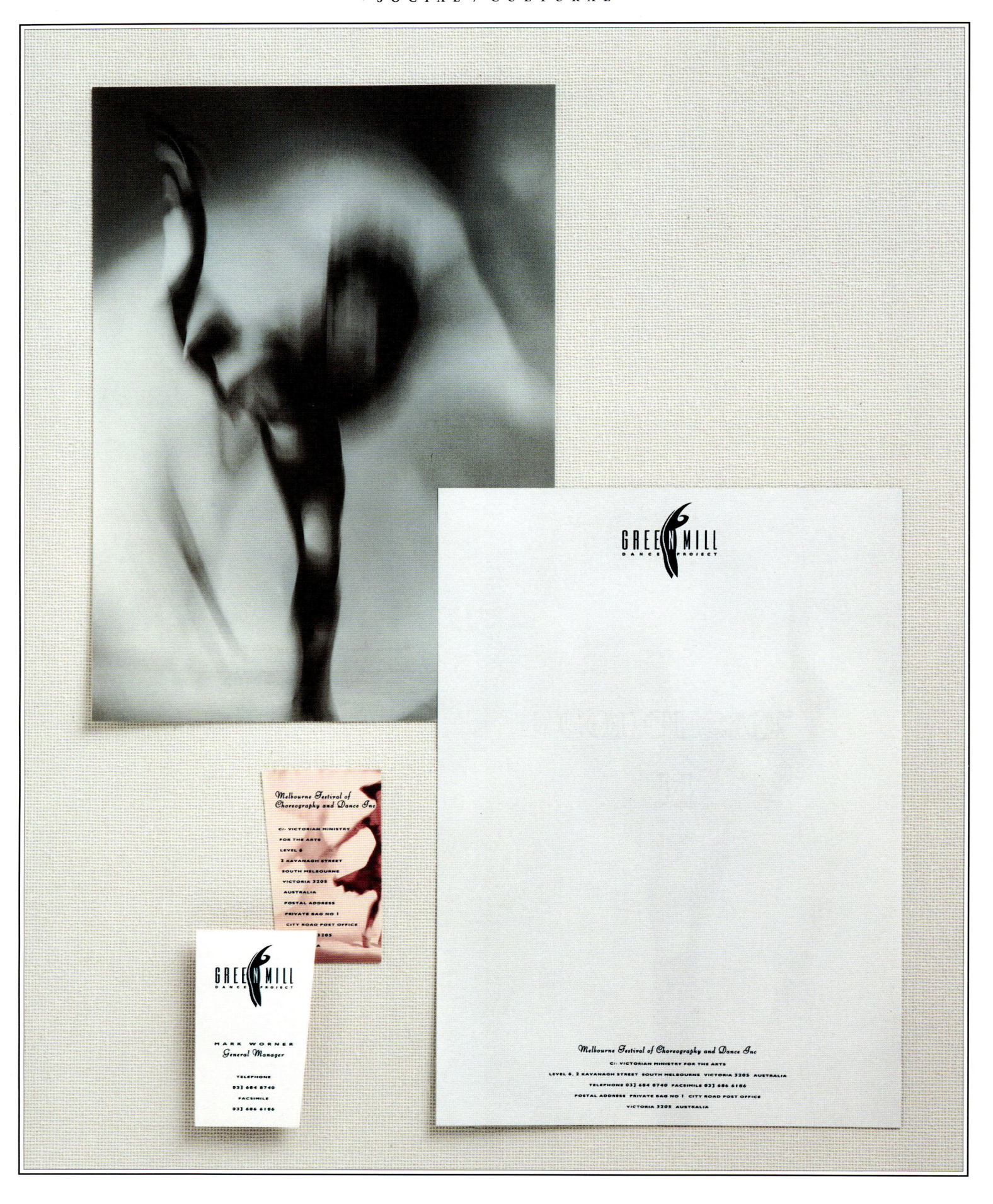

GREENMILL DANCE PROJECT Performing Arts and Dance Project   舞踏企画   AUSTRALIA 1993   AD, D: Richard Henderson   D: Lee McCartney   P: Tat-Mingh Yu   DF: FHA Design Australia

◆ SOCIAL / CULTURAL ◆

BARRY MACKAY SPORTS　Tennis Tournament　テニストーナメント　USA 1990　AD: Bill Cahan　D: Stuart Flake / Talin Gureghian　DF: Cahan & Assoc.

• SOCIAL / CULTURAL •

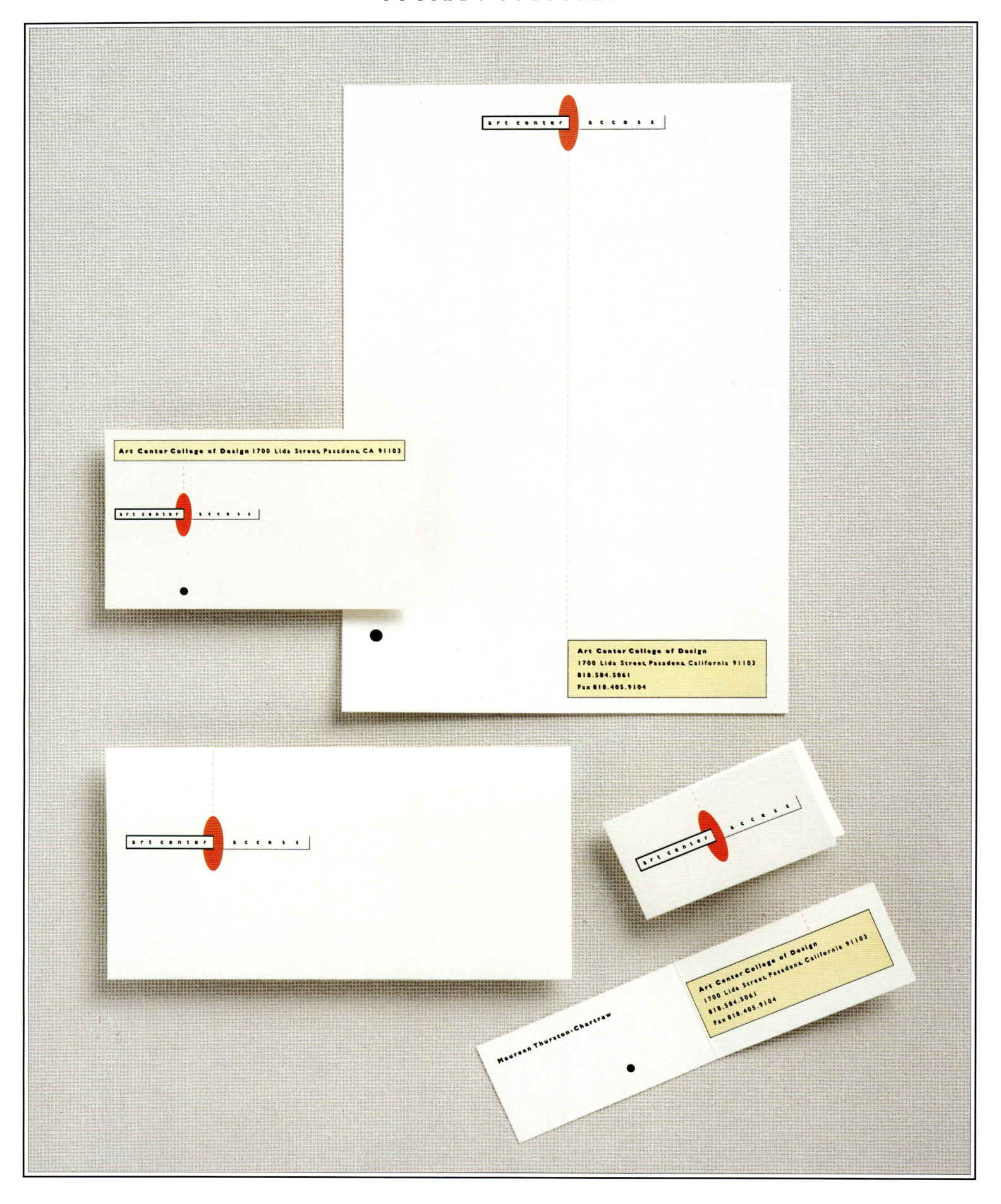

ART CENTER ACCESS, ART CENTER COLLEGE OF DESIGN   Art College   美術専門学校   USA   1992   AD, D: Rebeca Méndez   PRINTER: Star Plinting, Los Angeles, California

• SOCIAL / CULTURAL •

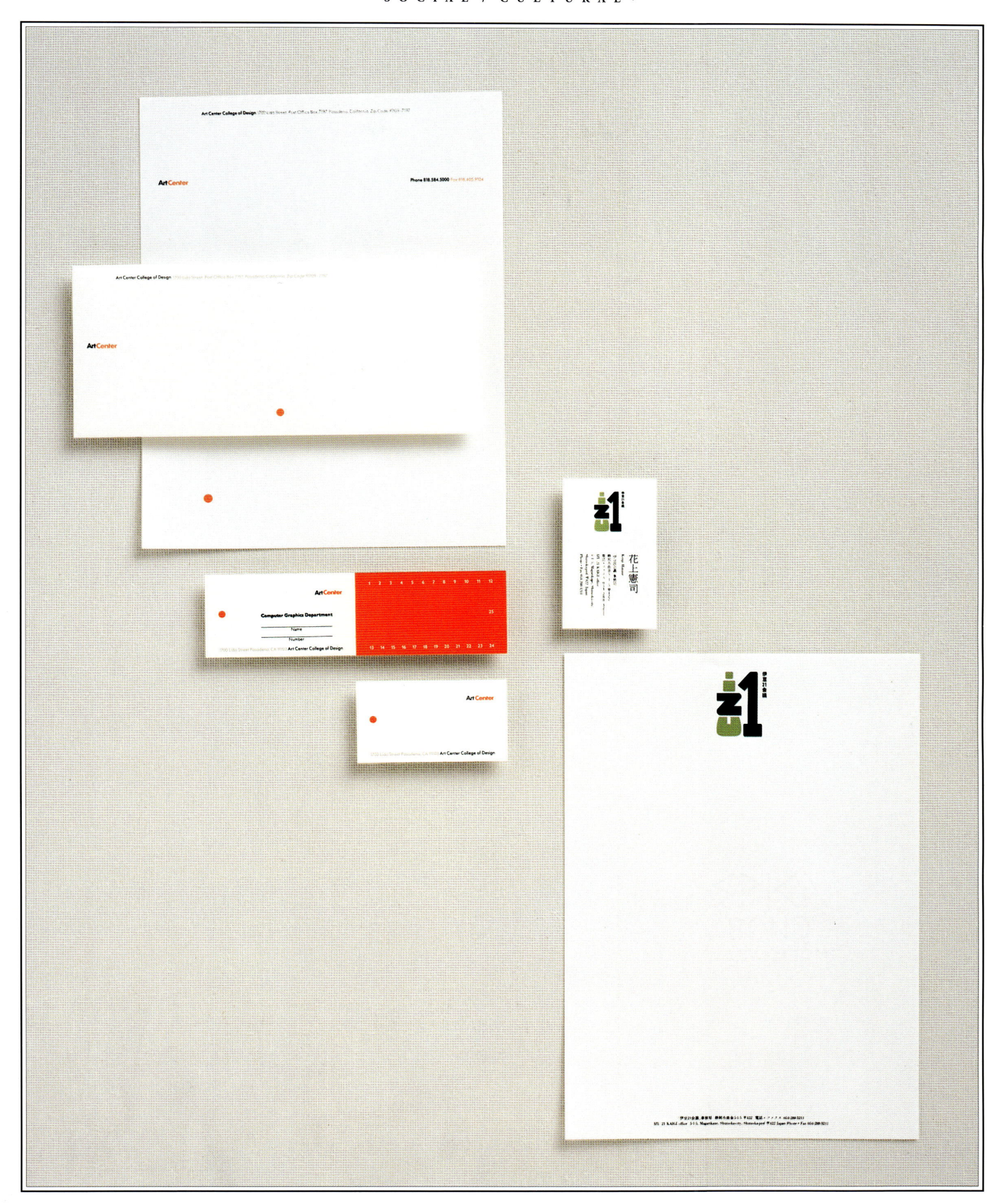

ART CENTER COLLEGE OF DESIGN   Art College   美術専門学校   USA 1990   AD, D: Rebeca Méndez   PRINTER: Typecraft., Pasadena, California
IZU 21 KAIGI   Regional Planning   伊豆半島全体の未来を考える会   JAPAN 1992   CD: Kenji Hanaue / Hiroshi Hasegawa   AD, D: Yoshiro Kajitani   D: Michiko Arakawa   DF: Kajitani Design Room

• SOCIAL / CULTURAL •

SHIRLEY GOODMAN RESOURCE CENTER Fashion Institute of Technology 科学技術のファッション専門学校 USA 1990
AD, D: Takaaki Matsumoto AD: Michael McGinn D: Mikio Sakai DF: M Plus M

◆ SPECIAL PROGRAM (Fax headers) ◆

• SPECIAL PROGRAM (Fax headers) •

QUADRANT RESEARCH & DEVELOPMENT LTD   Systems Software Research and Development   システムソフトウエアの研究開発   UK 1993
AD, D: The Designers Republic   DF: The Designers Republic
KINEMA MOON DESIGNING   Graphic Design   グラフィックデザイン   JAPAN 1993   AD: Yuichi Nakagawa   D: Sachiko Kitani   DF: Kinema Moon Designing

• SPECIAL PROGRAM (Fax headers) •

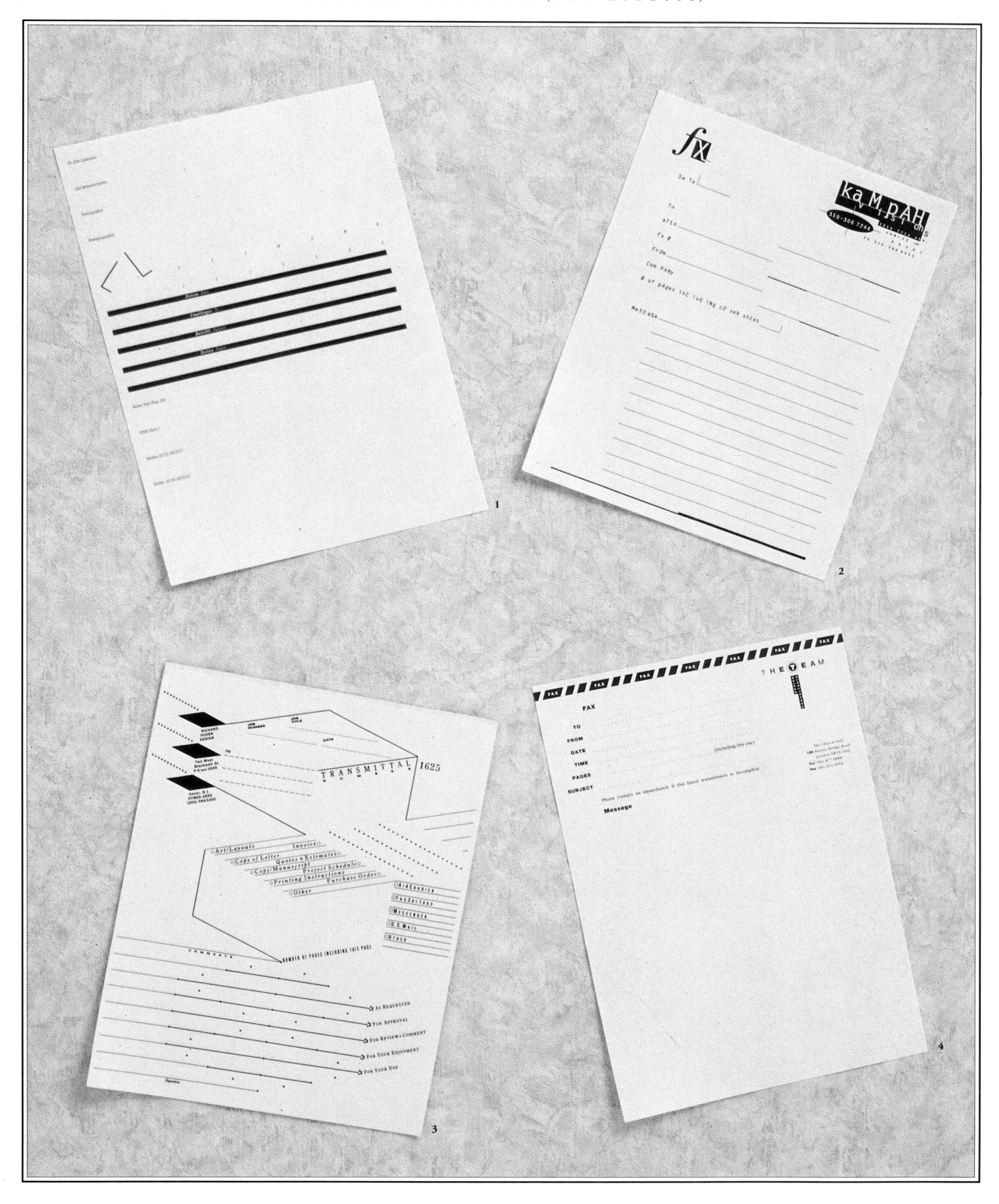

1. **DR. ELKE LUDEMANN** Sports-Science 運動科学研究 GERMANY 1991 AD, D: Detlef Behr DF: Detlef Behr, Graphik-Design
2. **KAMPAH VISIONS** Broadcast Design 放送設計デザイン USA 1993 AD, D: Flavio Kampah DF: Kampah Visions
3. **RICHARD PUDER DESIGN** Visual Communication Design 視覚伝達デザイン USA 1989 CD: Richard Puder D: Lee Grabarczyk DF: Richard Puder Design
4. **THE TEAM** Graphic Design グラフィックデザイン UK 1990 CD, D: Richard Ward DF: The Team

• SPECIAL PROGRAM (Fax headers) •

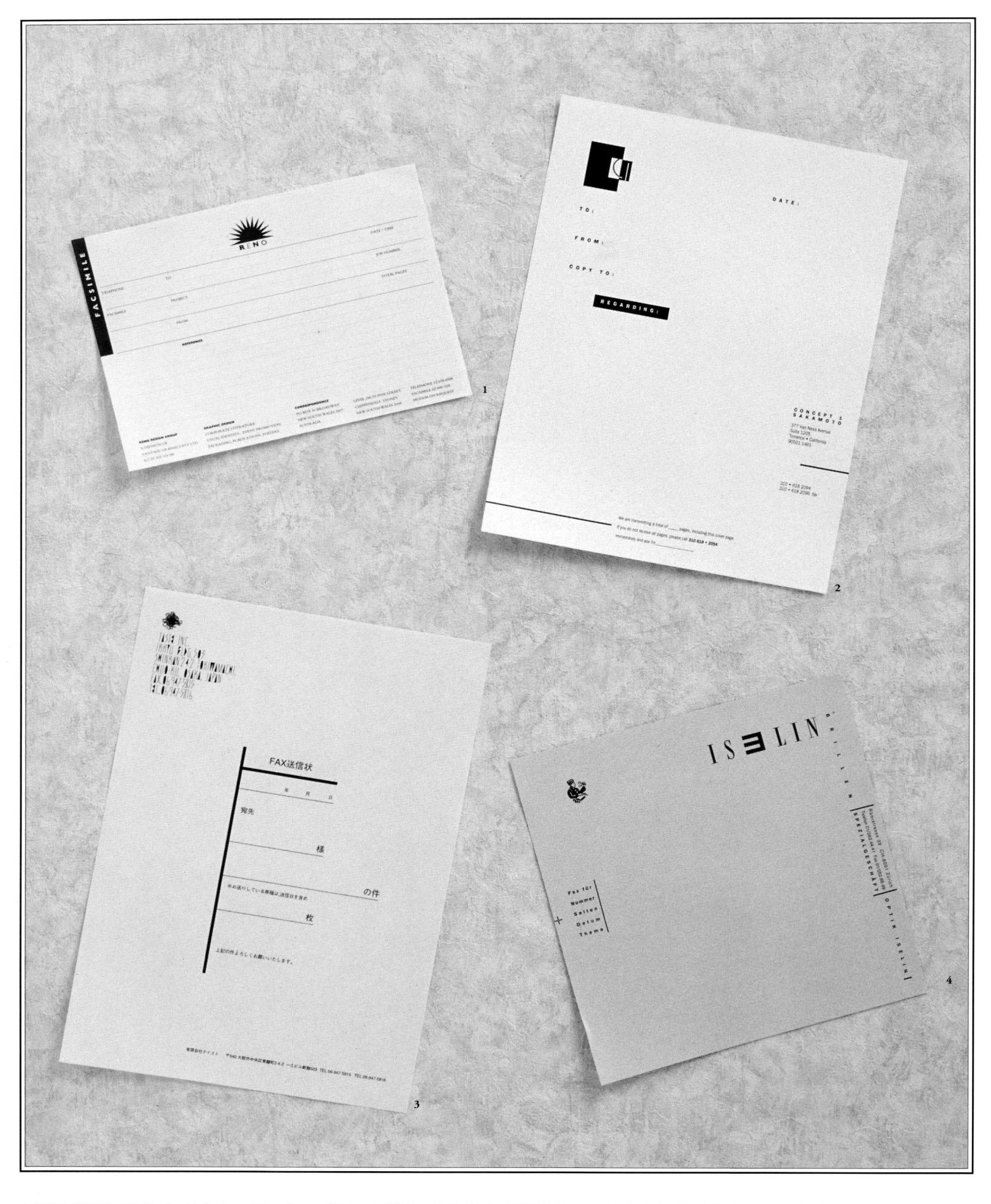

1. **RENO DESIGN GROUP**   Graphic Design and Consultancy   グラフィックデザイン、コンサルタント   AUSTRALIA   1990   AD, D: Graham Rendoth   CW: Reno Design Group   DF: Reno Design Group
2. **CONCEPT 1 / SAKAMOTO**   Jewelry Manufacturer   宝石製造   USA   1993   AD, D: Cindy Luck   DF: Luck Design
3. **TASTE INC.**   Graphic Design   グラフィックデザイン   JAPAN   1992   AD, D: Toshiyasu Nanbu
4. **OPTIK ISELIN**   Exclusive Retailer of Glasses   高級メガネ販売   SWITZERLAND   1991   AD, D, I: Christian Hügin   DF: Christian Hügin

• SPECIAL PROGRAM (Fax headers) •

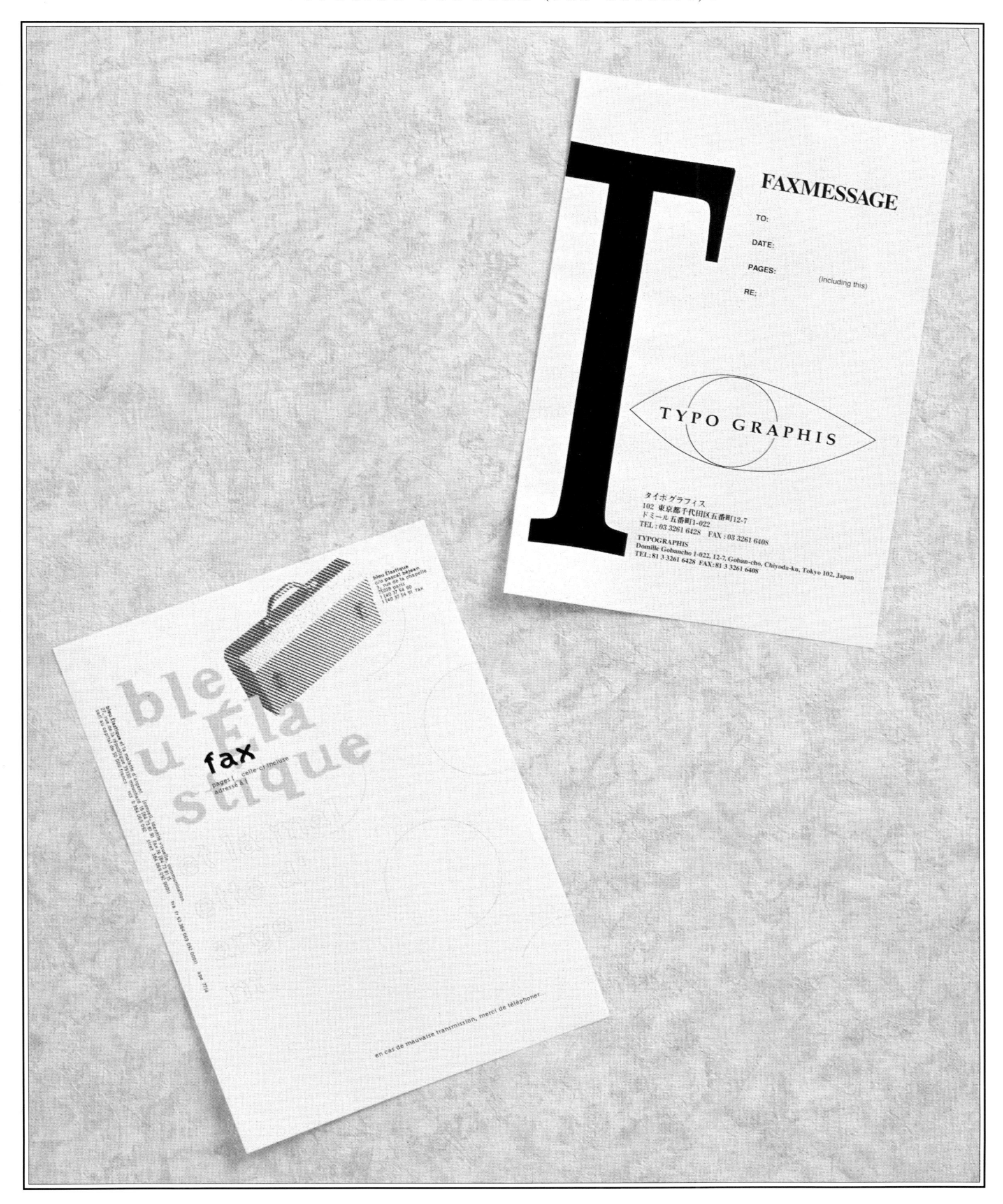

TYPO GRAPHIS Typography タイポグラフィ JAPAN 1992 AD, D: Tetsuyuki Kokin DF: Typographis

BLEU ÉLASTIQUE Design デザイン FRANCE 1993 AD, D: Pascal Béjean P: Gilles Marcodini CW: Bleu Élastique DF: Bleu Élastique

• SPECIAL PROGRAM (Fax headers) •

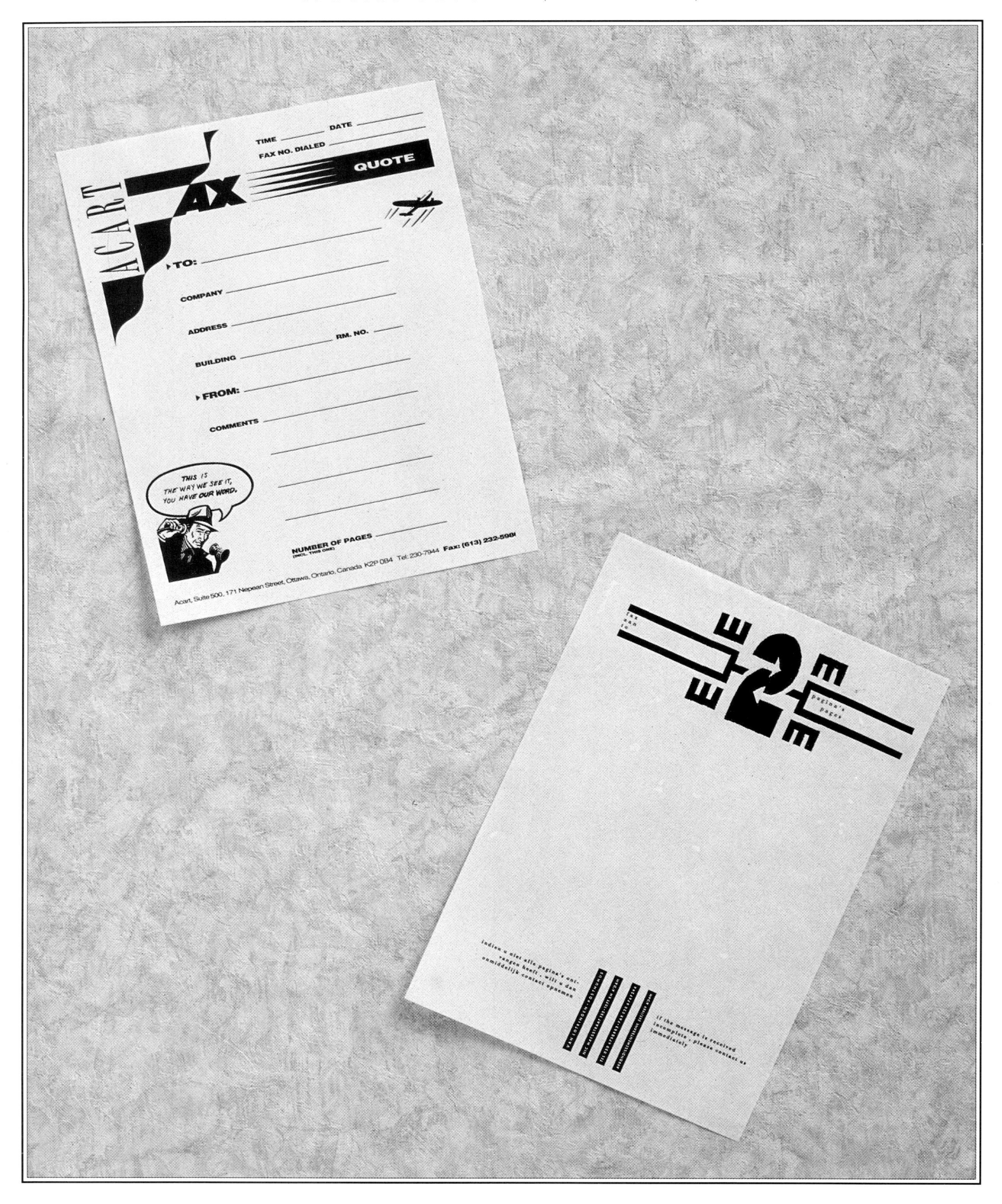

ACART GROUP OF COMPANIES   Graphics / Communication, Exhibits Service   グラフィックデザイン / 情報通信、展示サービス   CANADA 1990-1991
CD: John Staresinic   D, I: Ross Gervais   CW: Acart Team   DF: Acart Graphic Service
WALTER VAN LOTRINGEN / TINEKE POSTHUMUS   Freelance Illustrator / Art Historian   フリーランス・イラストレーター / 美術歴史学者   THE NETHERLANDS 1991
AD: Teun Anders VBAT   D: Marc Lochs   CW: Walter van Lotringen

◆ SPECIAL PROGRAM (Fax headers) ◆

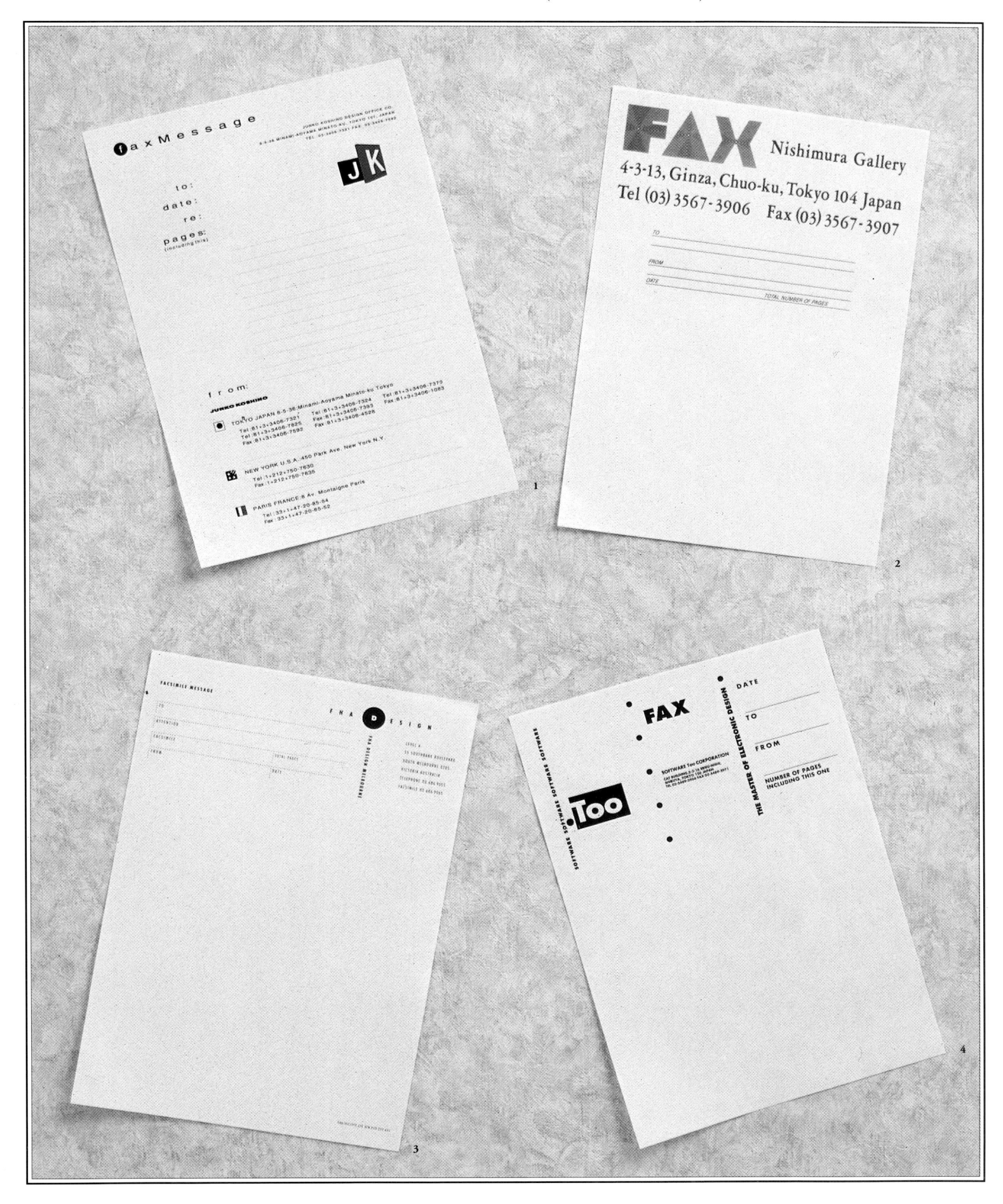

1. **JUNKO KOSHINO DESIGN OFFICE CO.** Apparel Maker アパレルメーカー JAPAN 1993 CD: Hiroyuki Suzuki AD: Junko Koshino D: Tetsuyuki Kokin DF: Typographis
2. **NISHIMURA GALLERY** Gallery 画廊 JAPAN 1991 D: Akihito Tsukamoto DF: Design Club
3. **FHA DESIGN** Graphic Design グラフィックデザイン AUSTRALIA 1993 AD, D: Richard Henderson D: Julia Jarvis DF: FHA Design Australia
4. **SOFTWARE TOO CORPORATION** Computer Related Service コンピューター関連ソフト・ハードウェアの輸入、販売、代理業 JAPAN 1991 AD: Naomi Enami D: Mariko Yamamoto DF: Propeller Art Works

• SPECIAL PROGRAM (Fax headers) •

NEVERNEVER ADRIAN Sportswear Manufacturer スポーツウエアメーカー USA 1991 AD, D: Brian Burchfield DF: Studio Seireeni
NICE Graphic Design グラフィックデザイン UK 1991 CD: Stephen Male / Neil Edwards / Richard Bonner Morgan D: Nice DF: Nice

◆ INDEXES ◆

INDEX OF CLIENTS

A
ABO ARCHITECTS 49
ACACIA AGENCY 95
ACART GROUP OF COMPANIES 214
AHA-JACEK BRETSZNAJDER 162
ALFALFA 53
ALL DIRECTIONS 185
ALLYSON ANTHONY 55
AMM.NE PROVINCIALE DI FERRARA 197
ANDY IP 60
ANNE-MARIE APPLIN 107
ARCHITECTO 158
ARMIN SCHNEIDER 168
ART CENTER COLLEGE OF DESIGN 192, 206, 207
ART DIRECTORS CLUB OF METROPOLITAN WASHINGTON 54
ART KANE 30
ARTS COUNCIL OF GREAT BRITAIN 201
AUDIO VISUAL ENTERPRISE CENTRE 96

B
BARNEY TABACH, AVID 180
BARRY MACKAY SPORTS 205
BARTHOLOMÄUS MOOSBRUGGER 155
b'BLUMENTHAL 182
BECKER-KORREKTUREN 165
BECKLEY IMPORTS, INC. 160
BERGMANN WASMER & ASSOCIATES 191
BLEU ÉLASTIQUE 213
BLIND SPOT, INC. 110
BOUNCE RECORDS 104
BOWHAUS 138
BRADFORD LAWTON DESIGN GROUP 89
BROOKS HOWARD 146

C
CAHAN & ASSOCIATES 44
CALLAHAN & COMPANY 35
CASTLE GREEN 70
CAVU DESIGN 74
CENTER FOR ORAL AND MAXILLOFACIAL SURGERY 190
CESAR RUBIO PHOTOGRAPHY 28
CHAMELEON INVESTIGATIONS, INC. 159
CHARLES S. ANDERSON DESIGN COMPANY 17
CHEZ LAHLOU 133
CHUCKIE-BOY RECORDS 92
CLIF SPARKMAN 48
COLLEGE POSTERS + PRINTS 140
COLOR CONTROL 174
CONCEPT 1 / SAKAMOTO 212
CONCEPT WORKS SHIGOTOBA INC. 77
CORPORATE WORLD RELOCATION 189
CREATIVE CLUB OF ATLANTA 57
CURATOR OFFICE INC. 183
CURRAN ART GLASS 149

D
DA VINCI GROEP 187
DALE F. STEELE 165
DAVID LOFTUS ILLUSTRATION 23
DAVID QUAY DESIGN 63
DAVID WARREN DESIGN 171
D. D. II KARAOKE 117
DESIGN LABORATORY 83
DESIGNERS COMPANY 11
DIVERSE HANDEL 119
DOUGLAS K. LARSON, D.D.S 160
DR. ELKE LUDEMANN 211
DR. GÜNTER LUDESCHER 173
DRUKKERI ELCO 147
DUBBIN & CO PRESENTATION CONSULTANTS 37

E
EAGLE LAKE ON ORCAS ISLAND 178
EDGE PHOTOGRAPHY 59
801 STEAK AND CHOP HOUSE 141
ELLEN ROSENBERG 41

ERWIN WIJNANDS & LEX BUNNIK 179
ESQUISSE INC. 15
EUROPEAN MARKETING DISTRIBUTION 188
EYE STUDIO 26

F
FACTORY 124
FHA DESIGN 48, 215
FIELD AND WALL PRODUCTIONS, INC. 109
FINGERPRINTS PHOTOGRAPHIC LIMITED 34
FORSYTHE DESIGN 45

G
GENQUI NUMATA 86-87
GERY ROEKENS / HET BURGER MEESTERS HUYS 129
GLENN HILLING 67
GOLF GROUP LTD. 167
GOLF MANAGEMENT INTERNATIONAL 170
GOOD PICTURES 113
GREENMILL DANCE PROJECT 204
GRZELAK BRYANT 156
GULLIVER CO., LTD. 24, 25, 80, 81
GWEN MACLAINE PONT 150

H
HIGGINS DESIGN 62
H. M. BRANDSTON & PARTNERS 40
HONG KONG SEIBU ENTERPRISE CO., LTD. 134
HOOGSTRATEN PARTNERS 161
HUNDRED INC. 84

I
I. A. BEDFORD 142
I COMME IMAGE 12
IDEAPAJA 172
IFF COMPANY INC. 76
INNOTEC GmbH 154
INTEGRUS ARCHITECTURE 191
IOWA HEALTH RESEARCH INSTITUTE 153
IZU 21 KAIGI 207

J
JAQUET PARQUET AG 148
JASPER CONRAN 122
JOAN GARCIA ARGELAGUET 139
JOE TRELEVEN 54
JOHN F. KILEY III CPA 163
JOHN SPOSATO DESIGN + ILLUSTRATION 88
JOYCE BOUTIQUE LIMITED 135
JOYCE PUBLISHING 97
JUNKO KOSHINO DESIGN OFFICE CO. 215
J. W. TUMBLES 196

K
KAB, INC. (RYUICHI SAKAMOTO) 176
KAMPAH VISIONS 211
KATRIN FUCHS 190
KEES KASANDER 92
KIMURA KOHKI CO., LTD. 127
KINEMA MOON DESIGNING 13, 210
KODAK PHOTO SERVICE 61
KOKI KOGEI INC. 166
KORAKOT SRIVIKORN 67
KOWALSKI DESIGNWORKS, INC. 82
KOZO TAKEUCHI 78
KRONEN AUDIO 93
KURTZ MANN 186

L
LA 4ÉME DIMENSION 94
LATCHEZAR BOYADJIEV 52
LE BATEAU FEU 203
LEO BURNETT 107
LEONARD CURRIE DESIGN 55
LILO OPERA 128
LIMAGE DANGEREUSE BV 64
LINDSTROM PHOTOGRAPHY 60
LITIGATION VIDEO (NORM LARSEN, PRES.) 111
LITTLE GOLD 144

M

MAHLUM & NORDFORS MCKINLEY GORDON 152
MARK OLDACH DESIGN 63
MARK ZINGARELLI 42
MARZENA 27
MCGUIRE WILHOITE 98
M. E. DESIGN, LOS ANGELES 49
MELIA DESIGN GROUP 18
MICHAEL HAZARD ARCHITECTS 66
MICHAEL LEVIN 36
MIKE SALISBURY COMMUNICATIONS 14
MIKI CO, LTD. 126
MISTER FIX-IT 158
MOBILER HAUSHILFEDIENST FELDKIRCH 197
MODERN DOG 90, 91
MOMENTUM FILMS 112
MORLA DESIGN 43

N
NBBJ 159
NEVERNEVER ADRIAN 216
NICE 216
NISHIMURA GALLERY 215
NUMBER ONE DESIGN OFFICE 50

O
OBUNSHA PACIFIC CORPORATION 116
OHIO ARTS COUNCIL 203
ONE REEL / SEATTLE ARTS COMMISSION 195
OPTIK ISELIN 136, 212
OWENS DESIGN COMPANY 68

P
PARADIGM HEALTH CORP 163
PAUL BARGEHR 169
PENDULUM DESIGN 29
PEPE ORBEIN + ASSOCIATES 69
PLAZA / VAN DER SCHANS 20-21
POWDER 131
PRIME PUBLISHING CO. 108
PRINT CRAFT, INC. 146
PRU REX-HASSAN 105

Q
QUADRANT RESEARCH & DEVELOPMENT LTD 184, 210

R
RADIO VISION INTERNATIONAL 99
RAY MASSEY PHOTOGRAPHY 22
REKTA REKLAM TASARIM 52
REMY PAGART 17
RENO DESIGN GROUP 16, 212
RETAIL PORTFOLIO GROUP 157
RICHARD PUDER DESIGN 211
RICK WAHLSTROM 40
RITA'S CATERING 115
ROBERT BERGMAN-UNGAR 39
ROMY SIEBER (MRS.) ZÜRICH 164
ROSS SUTHERLAND 143
RYOICHI SAITO 31

S
SAGEBRUSH PRODUCTIONS 101
SABINE MOSKAT 119
SAGMEISTER GRAPHICS VIENNA 46
SANWOOD STUDIO 96
SASCMA FASHION DESIGN 125
SEEGERS EN GOMBEER VORMGEVING 71
SHEFFIELD CITY COUNCIL'S RED TAPE STUDIOS 96
SHIN SUGINO PHOTOGRAPHY 32-33
SHINMURA SUISAN 147
SHIRLEY GOODMAN RESOURCE CENTER 208
SLEMAKER REPRESENTS 75
SMASH BOX 118
SOCIETY FOR ENVIRONMENTAL GRAPHIC DESIGN 69
SOFTWARE TOO CORPORATION 105, 215
SPARE, TENGLER, KAPLAN & BISCHEL 157
SPORTS TURF DYNAMICS 181
SQUARE ONE PRESCHOOL 194
STAND 167

STEWART TILGER 51
STIL + BLÜTE, SILVIA RIEMANN + UTE REUSSENZEHN 130
STREAMLINE CORPORATE PLANNERS 121
STREAMLINE GRAPHICS 118
STUBENRAUCH + SIMON 106
STUDIO SEIREENI 41
SUNSET DECKS 114

T
TADEUSZ PIECHURA 61
TAKEO CO., LTD. 134, 137
TASTE INC. 79, 212
THE BECKETY PAPER COMPANY 145
THE CENTER FOR FAMILIES AND CHILDREN 201
THE DESIGN OFFICE, INC. 58
THE DESIGN OFFICE OF WONG & YEO 19
THE DESIGNERS REPUBLIC 10
THE HIVELY AGENCY 106
THE KENWOOD GROUP 102
THE KYOTO HOTEL LTD. 139
THE OLIVE 114
THE TEAM 211
THE WATER COMPANY 100
TOHTORE CO., LTD. 177
TOM SCHIERLITZ 47
TSUYOKATSU KUDO 85
TYPOGRAPHIS 213

U
UNIVERSITEIT UTRECHT 200
UNIVERSITY OF CALIFORNIA, BERKELEY 198
UP & RUNNING, INC. 177
UWE STEINMAYER 62

V
VAN WALSUM MANAGEMENT 151
VANDAMME REPRESENTS 73
VAUGHN WEDEEN CREATIVE 22
VAZARA 132
VELOCITY DEVELOPMENT CORPORATION 103
V. FRANK, AIA 162
VIANSA WINERY 120
VIÑA VALORIA CELLAR 123

W
WALTER VAN LOTRINGEN / TINEKE POSTHUMUS 72, 214
WARP RECORDS 97
WATERS DESIGN ASSOCIATES, INC. 65
WEIDEMAFONDS 202
WELLESLEY COLLEGE MUSEUM 193
WESTERN REGIONAL GREEK CONFERENCE 199

Y
YABU PUSHELBERG 38
YOUNG PRESIDENT'S ORGANIZATION 175

Z
ZIMMERMANN CROWE DESIGN 56
ZONK, INC. 133
Z-PIX, INC. 68

INDEX OF SUBMITORS

A
A. B. Vos 150
Acart Graphic Services Inc. 214
Alan Chan Design Company 97, 116, 117, 134, 135
Andy Ip 60
Art Chantry Design 42, 92, 101
Atelier Tadeusz Piechura 61, 162

B
Barnstorming Designs 163
BBV 164
Bleu Élastique 213
Bradford Lawton Design Group 89
Britton Design 120

C
Cabra Diseño 28
Cahan & Assoc. 44, 157, 205
Carmen Peña / Provenio Design Studio 123
Cavu Design 74
Charles S. Anderson Design Company 17, 68, 111, 146
Chloe Peppas 41
Christian Hügin 136, 148, 212
Clifford Stoltze Design 69
Concept Works Shigotoba Inc. 77
Concrete 41, 167

D
David Loftus Illustration 22, 23
David Roffey Design 181
David Quay Design 63
David Warren Design 49, 66, 171, 191
Dedato 100, 104, 147
Design Club 215
Designers Company 11
Detlef Behr, Graphik-design Agd 182, 211
Douglas Design Inc. 126

E
Egartner Grafik Design Gda 190
Evenson Design Group 118, 146
Eye Studio 26

F
FHA DESIGN 48, 204, 215
Forsythe Design 45

G
Gail Rigelhaupt 201
Genqui Numata 86-87
Glenn Hilling 34, 37, 67

H
Heter-O-Doxy Protprast 127
Higgins Design 62
Hornall Anderson Design Works, Inc. 51, 152, 178, 190, 191
Hundred Inc. 84

I
I Comme Image 12, 17, 94, 95, 203
Iff Graphics 76
Iva Frank Graphic Design 52, 162, 165

J
John Sposato 88
Joseph Baratelli Design 75

K
Kajitani Design Room 78, 132, 207
Kampah Visions 211
Kan Tai-keung Design & Associates Ltd. 108
KBO & R Design 125, 129, 161, 179
Keisuke Unosawa 177
Kenichi Samura 50
Kinema Moon Designing 13, 210
Kowalski Design Works, Inc. 82, 114
Kurt Dornig Grafik Design 119, 154, 173, 188

L
Lauren Smith Design 60, 160
Leo Burnett Hong Kong 107
Leonard Currie Design 55
Limage Dangereuse Br 64
Luck Design 212

M
M Plus M Incorporated 208
Marc Lochs 72, 214
Margo Chase Design 99, 118, 138
Mark Oldach Design 63, 115, 149
McCool & Company 54
Melia Design Group 18, 48, 57
Michael Levin 36
Michael Nash Associates 122
Midnight Oil Studios 143
Miho 30
Mike Salisbury Communications 14
Modern Dog 90, 91, 98
Morla Design 40, 43, 55, 113

N
Nakatsuka Daisuke Inc. 139
NBBJ 159, 195
Nedda Bonini 197
Nice 216
Norito Shinmura 147

O
Owens Design Company 68

P
Pendulum Design 29
Pepe Orbein + Associates 69
Peter Bradford and Associates 109, 159
Peter Haythornthwaite Design 59
Plaza Ontwerpers 20-21
plus design inc. 193
Powder Co.,Ltd 131
Proforma Rotterdam 200
Propeller Art Works Co.,Ltd 105, 215

R
Rebeca Méndez 49, 192, 206, 207
Rec 2nd 166
Rekta Reklam Tasarim 52
Reno Design Group 16, 156, 212
Richard Poulin Design Group Inc. 40
Richard Puder Design 211
Richardson or Richardson 112, 167, 170, 194, 196
Rick Eiber Design 174
Rickabaugh Graphics 145
Robert Bergman-Ungar Art Direction 27, 39, 110, 176

S
Sabin Design 133
Sagmeister Graphics 46, 47, 144, 168
Samenwerkende Ontwerpers 187, 202
Sayles Graphic Design 70, 141, 142, 153, 160, 180, 198, 199
Seegers En Gombeer Vormgeving 71
Sigi Ramoser 61, 155, 169, 197
Software Too Corporation 105, 215
Sommese Design 158
Stefanie Choi 189
Steinmayer Grafik 62
Stubenrauch + Simon 96, 106
Studio Seireeni 114, 216
Supon Design Group, Inc. 54, 119

T
Taste Inc. 79, 212
Tatsuomi Majima 15, 24, 25, 31, 80, 81
Taylor & Browning Design Associates 107
Teresa Roriras 53, 67, 105, 139
Terrelonge Design Inc. 32-33, 38, 157, 186
The Design Office, Inc. 58
The Design Office of Wong & Yeo 19, 102, 103
The Designers Republic 10, 96, 97, 133, 140, 184, 185, 201, 210
The Dunlavey Studio, Inc. 121
The Hively Agency 106, 158
The Studio Tokyo Japan,Inc. 81
The Team 151, 211
Trust Corporate Culture GmbH 124, 128, 130, 165
Tsuyokatsu Kudo 83, 85, 134, 137
T. Y. D. Inc. 183
Typographis 213, 215

V
Van Den Beginne BV 92
Vaughn Wedeen Creative, Inc. 22, 93
Viktorno Design Oy 172

W
Waters Design Associates, Inc. 65, 175, 203

Y
Yanovick & Associates 35
Youngblood, Sweat & Tears 177

Z
Zimmermann Crowe Design 56, 73, 163

BUSINESS STATIONERY GRAPHICS 2

Art Director, Designer

Sinji Ikenoue

Editor

Kaori Shibata

Photographer

Kuniharu Fujimoto

Business Manager

Masato Ieshiro

English Translator

Write Away Co., Ltd.

Thanks to

Clive Avins

Kaoru Endo

Publisher

Shingo Miyoshi

1994年2月20日初版第1版発行

発行所　ピエ・ブックス

〒170 東京都豊島区駒込4-14-6-407

TEL: 03-3949-5010　FAX: 03-3949-5650

© 1994 P·I·E BOOKS

製版　（株）飛来社

Plate Making in Japan by Try Sha Co..Ltd.

Printed and Bound in Hong Kong by Everbest Printing Co..Ltd.

本書の収録内容の無断転載、複写、引用等を禁じます。

落丁・乱丁はお取り替え致します。

ISBN 4-938586-48-7 C3070

P·I·E Books, as always, has several new and ambitious graphic book projects in the works which will introduce a variety of superior designs from Japan and abroad. Currently we are planning the collection series detailed below. If you have any graphics which you consider worthy for submission to these publications, please fill in the necessary information on the inserted questionnaire postcard and forward it to us. You will receive a notice when the relevant project goes into production.

REQUEST FOR SUBMISSIONS

- **A.** Postcard Graphics
- **B.** Advertising Greeting Cards
- **C.** Brochure & Pamphlet Collection
- **D.** Poster Graphics
- **E.** Book Cover and Editorial Design
- **F.** Corporate Image Design
- **G.** Business Card and Letterhead Graphics
- **H.** Calendar Graphics
- **I.** Packaging and Wrapping Graphics

ピエ・ブックスでは、今後も新しいタイプのグラフィック書籍の出版を目指すとともに、国内外の優れたデザインを幅広く紹介していきたいと考えております。今後の刊行予定として下記のコレクション・シリーズを企画しておりますので、作品提供していただける企画がございましたら、挟み込みのアンケートハガキに必要事項をご記入の上お送り下さい。企画が近づきましたらそのつど案内書をお送りいたします。

作 品 提 供 の お 願 い

- **A.** ポストカード・グラフィックス
- **B.** アドバタイジング・グリーティングカード
- **C.** ブローシュア＆パンフレット・コレクション
- **D.** ポスター・グラフィックス
- **E.** ブックカバー＆エディトリアル・デザイン
- **F.** コーポレイト・イメージ＆ロゴマーク・デザイン
- **G.** ビジネスカード＆レターヘッド・グラフィックス
- **H.** カレンダー・グラフィックス
- **I.** パッケージ＆ラッピング・グラフィックス

Comme toujours, P·I·E Books a dans ses ateliers plusieurs projets de livres graphiques neufs et ambitieux qui introduiront une gamme de modèles supérieurs en provenance du Japon et de l'étranger. Nous prévoyons en ce moment la série de collections détaillée cidessous. Si vous êtes en possession d'un graphique que vous jugez digne de soumettre à ces publications, nous vous prions de remplir les informations nécessaires sur l'étiquette à renvoyer située à la carte postale questionnaire insérée et de nous la faire parvenir. Vous recevrez un avis lorsque le projet correspondant passera à la production.

DEMANDE DE SOUMISSIONS

- **A.** Graphiques pour cartes postales
- **B.** Cartes de voeux publicitaires
- **C.** Collection de brochures et de pamphlets
- **D.** Graphiques sur affiche
- **E.** Designs de couverture de livre et d'éditorial
- **F.** Designs de logo d'image de société
- **G.** Graphiques pour en-têtes et cartes de visite
- **H.** Graphiques pour calendrier
- **I.** Graphiques pour emballage et paquetage

Wie immer hat P·I·E Books einige neue anspruchsvolle Grafikbücher in Arbeit, die eine Vielzahl von hervorragenden Designs aus Japan und anderen Ländern vorstellen werden. Momentan planen wir eine Serie mit den nachfolgend aufgeführten Themen. Wenn Sie grafische Darstellungen besitzen, von denen Sie meinen, daß sie in diese Veröffentlichung aufgenommen werden könten, geben Sie uns bitte die nötigen Informationen auf der entsprechenden Antwortseite am füllen Sie die beigelegte Antwortkarte aus und schicken Sie sie an uns. Wir werden Sie benachrichtigen, wenn das entsprechende Projekt in Arbeit geht.

AUFFORDERUNG ZU MITARBEIT

- **A.** Postkarten-Grafik
- **B.** Werbe-Grußkarten
- **C.** Zusammenstellung von Broschüren und Druckschriften
- **D.** Postergrafik
- **E.** Bucheinbände und redaktionelles Design
- **F.** Corporate-Image-Logo-Design
- **G.** Visitenkarten und Briefkopf-Grafik
- **H.** Kalendergrafik
- **I.** Grafik auf Verpackungen und Verpackungsmaterial

THE P·I·E COLLECTION

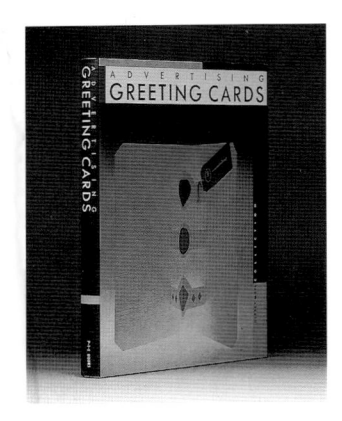

ADVERTISING GREETING CARDS 1
Pages: 224(144 in color) ¥15,000
業種別ダイレクトメールの集大成
A collection of more than 500 direct mail pieces selected from thousands used throughout Japan. Cards were selected for their distinctive design and include 3-D pop-ups, special die-cuts, folds and embossings.

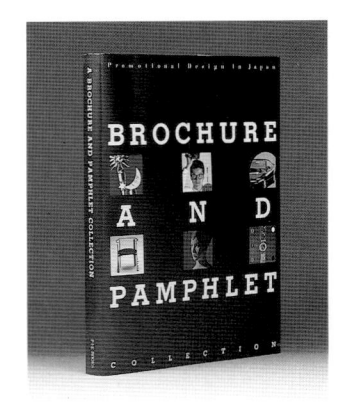

BROCHURE & PAMPHLET COLLECTION 1
Pages: 224(144 in color) ¥15,000
業種別カタログ・コレクション
Here are hundreds of the best brochures and pamphlets from Japan.
This collection will make a valuable sourcebook for anyone involved in corporate identity advertising and graphic design.

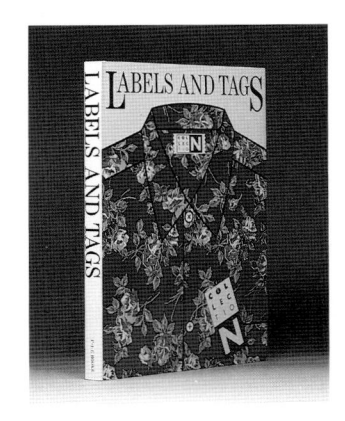

LABELS AND TAGS
Pages: 224(192 in color) ¥15,000
ファッションのラベル&タグ・コレクション
Over 1,600 garment labels representing 450 brands produced in Japan are included in this full-color collection.

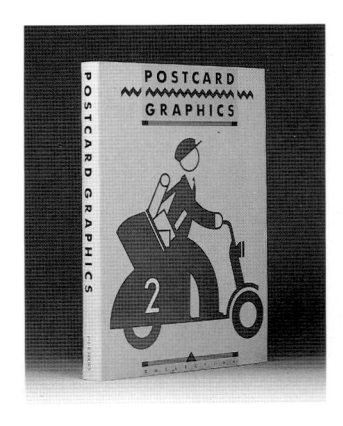

POSTCARD GRAPHICS 2
Pages: 240(208 in color) ¥16,000
好評！業種別ポストカードの第2弾
Here are 1,500 promotional postcards created by Japan's top design talent. A wide range of clients are represented including 120 fashion houses and 90 major retailers. Presented in striking full color.

BUSINESS CARD GRAPHICS 1
Pages: 256(160 in color) ¥16,000
世界の名刺&ショップカード集大成
Over 1,200 business cards are presented in this international collection.
Created by 500 of the world's top design firms, designers will discover a wealth of new ideas in this remarkable collection.

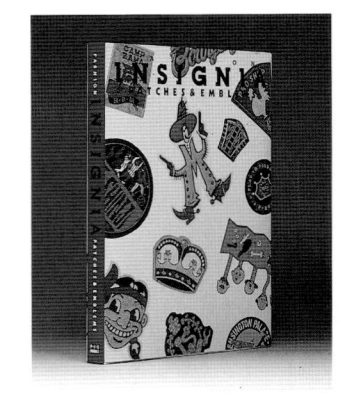

FASHION INSIGNIA
Pages: 224(208 in color) ¥16,000
ファッションのワッペン・コレクション
One thousand full-color emblems have been gathered in this beautiful and sometimes playful collection.
The great variety of color and shape demonstrates the versatility of embroidery art.

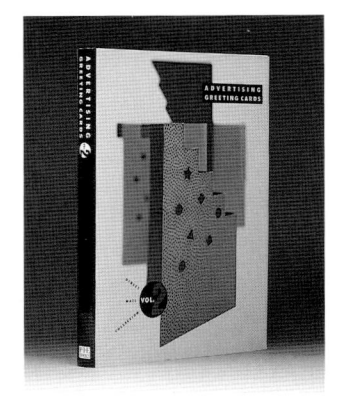

ADVERTISING GREETING CARDS 2
Pages: 224(176 in color) ¥16,000
世界のダイレクトメール・コレクション
500 visually remarkable works representing a variety of businesses.
Pieces include new product announcements, invitation cards and direct mail envelopes. An excellent image bank for graphic designers.

BROCHURE DESIGN FORUM 1
Pages: 224(192 in color) ¥15,000
世界のカタログ・コレクション
A large collection of international brochures from a variety of business categories. Showcases more than 250 eye-catching works.

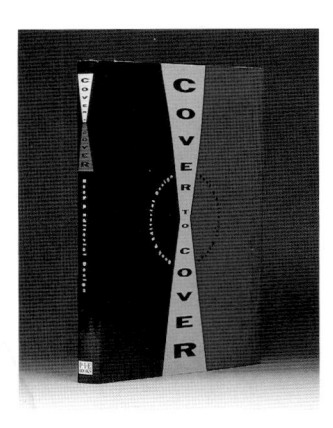

COVER TO COVER
Pages: 240(176 in color) ¥17,000
世界のブック&エディトリアル・デザイン
The latest trends in book and magazine design are illustrated with over 1,000 creative works by international firms.

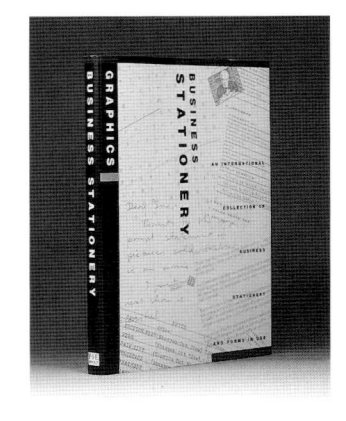

BUSINESS STATIONERY GRAPHICS 1
Pages: 224(192 in color) ¥15,000
世界のレターヘッド・コレクション
Creatively designed letterheads, business cards, memo pads, and other business forms and documents are included this international collection.

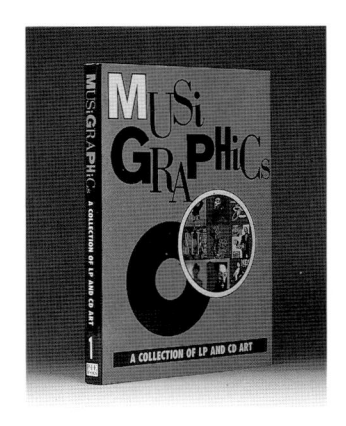

MUSIGRAPHICS 1
Pages: 224(192 in color) ¥16,000
世界のLP&CDグラフィックス
A collection of more than 600 of the world's most outstanding CD and LP covers, featuring design for all musical genres.

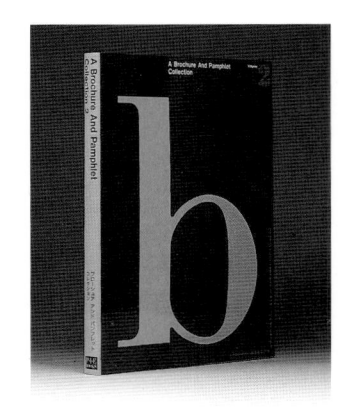

BROCHURE & PAMPHLET COLLECTION 2
Pages: 224(192 in color) ¥15,000
業種別カタログ・コレクション、第2弾
Features a selection of 1,000 brochures and pamphlets covering a wide range of products from Japan. The value of brochures in visual communication is demonstrated in this dazzling collection.

THE P·I·E COLLECTION

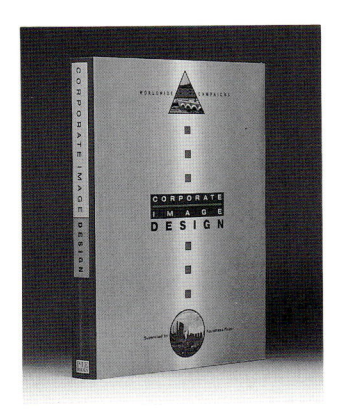

CORPORATE IMAGE DESIGN
Pages: 336(272 in color) ¥16,000
世界の業種別CI・ロゴマーク
This collection presents the best corporate identity projects from around the world. Creative and effective designs from top international firms are featured in this valuable source book.

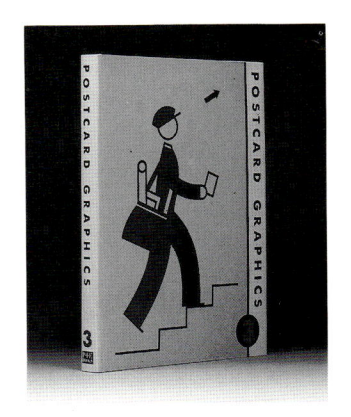

POSTCARD GRAPHICS 3
Pages: 232(208 in color) ¥16,000
世界の業種別ポストカード・コレクション
Volume 3 in the series presents more than 1,200 promotional postcards in dazzling full color. Top designers from the world over have contributed to this useful image bank of ideas.

GRAPHIC BEAT London / Tokyo 1 & 2
Pages: 224(208 in color) ¥16,000
音楽とグラフィックのコラボレーション
1,500 music-related graphic works from 29 of the hottest designers in Tokyo and London. Features Malcolm Garrett, Russell Miles, Tadanori Yokoo, Neville Brody, Vaughn Oliver and others.

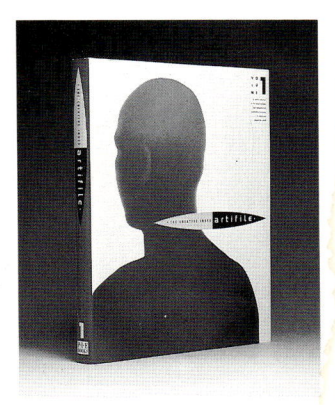

The Creative Index ARTIFILE 1
Pages: 224(Full color) ¥12,500
実力派プロダクション104社の作品集
Showcases the best works from 104 graphic studios in Japan and abroad. A variety of fields included such as advertising design, corporate identity, photography and illustration.

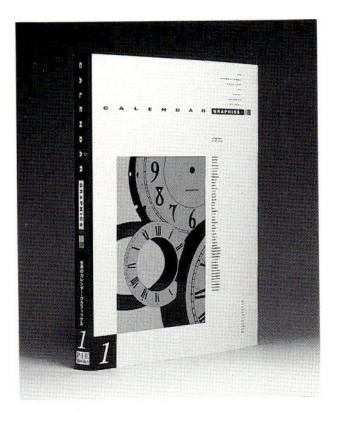

CALENDAR GRAPHICS
Pages: 224(192 in color) ¥16,000
世界のカレンダー・グラフィックス
An exciting collection of creatively designed calendars from around the world. A wide variety of styles included such as poster, book and 3-D calendars. Clients range from large corporations to retail shops.

BUSINESS CARD GRAPHICS 2
Pages: 224(192 in color) ¥16,000
世界の名刺&ショップカード、第2弾
This latest collection presents 1,000 creative cards from international designers. Features hundreds of cards used in creative fields such as graphic design and architecture.

T-SHIRT GRAPHICS
Pages: 224(192 in color) ¥16,000
世界のTシャツ・グラフィックス
This unique collection showcases 700 wonderfully creative T-Shirt designs from the world's premier design centers. Grouped according to theme, categories include sports, casual, designer and promotional shirts among others.

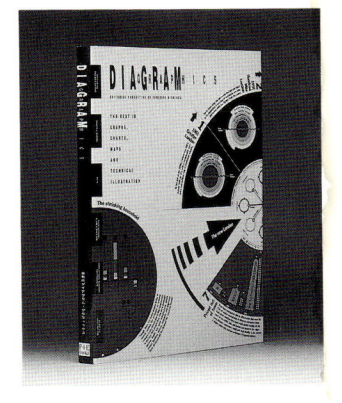

DIAGRAM GRAPHICS
Pages: 224(192 in color) ¥16,000
世界のダイアグラム・デザインの集大成
Hundreds of unique and lucid diagrams, charts, graphs, maps and technical illustrations from leading international design firms. Variety of media represented including computer graphics.

SPECIAL EVENT GRAPHICS
Pages: 224(192 in color) ¥16,000
世界のイベント・グラフィックス特集
This innovative collection features design elements from concerts, festivals, fashion shows, symposiums and more. International works include posters, tickets, flyers, invitations and various premiers.

PACKAGING DESIGN & GRAPHICS 1
Pages: 224(192 in color) ¥16,000
世界の業種別パッケージ・デザイン
An international collection featuring 400 creative and exciting package designs from renowned designers.

RETAIL IDENTITY GRAPHICS
Pages: 208(176 in color) ¥14,800
世界のショップ・グラフィックス
This visually exciting collection showcases the identity design campaigns of restaurants, bars, shops and various other retailers. Wide variety of pieces are featured including business cards, signs, menus, bags and hundreds more.

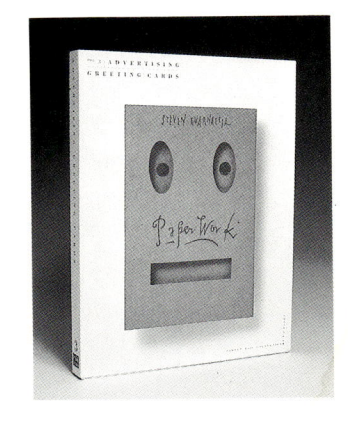

ADVERTISING GREETING CARDS 3
Pages: 224(176 in color) ¥16,000
世界のダイレクトメール集大成、第3弾
The best-selling series continues with this collection of elegantly designed advertising pieces from a wide variety of categories. This exciting image bank of ideas will interest all graphic designers and direct mail specialists.

THE P·I·E COLLECTION

TYPODIRECTION IN JAPAN 4
Pages: 254(183 in color) ¥17,000
年鑑 日本のタイポディレクション '92
314 award-winning works of outstanding typographical art from Japan and abroad. Included, you will find up-to-the-minute examples of concept-development works and previously unpublished typefaces from top art dirctors and graphic designers.

NEW TYPO GRAPHICS
Pages: 224(192 in color) ¥16,000
世界の最新タイポグラフィ・コレクション
New and innovative typographical works gathered from top designers around the world. A wide variety of type applications are shown including posters, brochures, CD jackets, calendars, book designs and more.

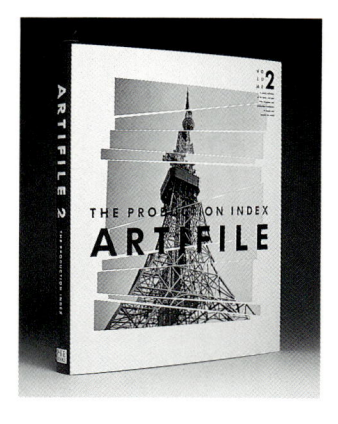

The Production Index ARTIFILE 2
Pages: 244(240 in color) ¥13,500
活躍中！最新プロダクション年鑑、第２弾
A design showcase featuring the best works from 115 graphic design studios, photographers, and creators in Japan. Works shown include print advertisements, corporate identity pieces, commercial photography and illustration.

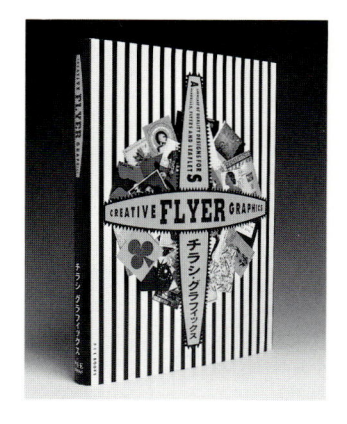

CREATIVE FLYER GRAPHICS
Pages:224(176 in color) ¥16,000
チラシ・グラフィックス
Features about 500 rigorously screened flyers and leaflets. You see what superior graphics can accomplish on a single sheet of paper. This is an invaluable reference to all your advertising production for years to come.

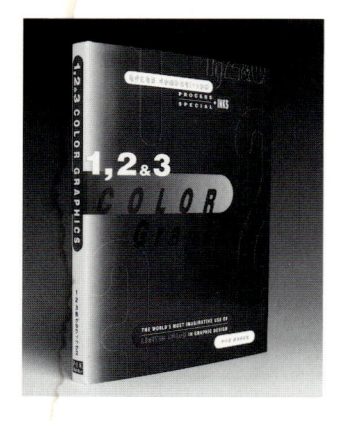

1・2 & 3 COLOR GRAPHICS
Pages:208(Full Color) ¥16,000
１・２・３色 グラフィックス
See about 300 samples of 1,2 & 3 color artworks that are so expressive they often surpass the impact of full 4 color reproductions. This is a very important book that will expand the possibilities of your design works in the future.

LABELS AND TAGS 2
Pages:224(192 in color) ¥16,000
世界のラベル&タグ・コレクション　2
This long-awaited second volume features 1500samples representing 400 top name-brands from around the world.

BROCHURE DESIGN FORUM 2
Pages:224(176 in color) ¥16,000
世界の最新カタログ・コレクション　2
Features 70 businesses and 250 reproductions for a complete overview of the latest and best in brochure design.

カタログ・新刊のご案内について
総合カタログ・新刊案内をご希望の方は、はさみ込みのアンケートはがきを
ご返送いただくか、７２円切手同封の上、ピエ・ブックス宛にお申し込み下さい。